LEAAM

Socio. ⋯ ⋯ Curriculum

Theology in Dialogue Series
Series Editor: Ian Markham

The Theology in Dialogue series is an internationally supported response to a pressing need to explore the relationship between theology and the different, ostensibly secular, academic disciplines which appear within the degree programmes of colleges and universities. It has been developed by The Council of Church and Associated Colleges (CCAC), a network of UK-based colleges and universities which have Church foundations.

Each volume begins with a chapter and a reply, providing a thoughtful justification for the interaction of theology and each subject. This is followed by a theoretical analysis of this interaction, and a range of case studies illustrating the difference this makes in the classroom. All volumes contain contributions from the most highly respected scholars in their field.

Other books in the series:

English Literature, Theology and the Curriculum edited by Liam Gearon
The grand narrative of theology and the many narratives of literature have interacted with complex and culturally enriching results over the centuries. This volume provides an enlivened, interdisciplinary debate between the fields of English literature and theology. The analysis of this textual dynamic ranges from varied, historical case studies in theology and literature, to practical concerns centring upon effective models of curriculum innovation, especially, but not exclusively, in higher education.

Spirituality and the Curriculum edited by Adrian Thatcher
'Spirituality' and 'spiritual development' are increasingly widespread concepts, particularly within the pastoral profession of education. In this volume, leading theologians and educationalists discuss spirituality from the point of view of theology, its home discipline, and apply the results of their enquiries to the curriculum in colleges and schools.

Theology in Dialogue Series
Series Editor: Ian Markham

Sociology, Theology and the Curriculum

Edited by Leslie J. Francis

CASSELL
London and New York

Cassell

Wellington House, 125 Strand, London WC2R 0BB
370 Lexington Avenue, New York, NY 10017-6550

© Leslie J. Francis and the contributors 1999

First published 1999

British Library Cataloguing-in-Publication Data
A catalogue record for this book is available from the British Library.

ISBN 0-304-70485-7

Typeset by BookEns Ltd, Royston, Herts.
Printed and bound in Great Britain by Biddles Ltd,
Guildford and King's Lynn

Contents

Contents

Series Editor's Foreword

One of the central questions facing theological discourse must be its relationship with other discourses in the academy. For the academy this issue is acute. The twin pressures of secularization and plurality have inhibited theological reflection; theology has been confined to a 'department'; the result being that students on different degree programmes do not explore the overall framework and assumptions of their study. Certain fundamental value questions are entirely neglected.

This series is a challenge to the confinement of theological reflection to a single department. We believe that a full and rounded education ought to provide the space for wide-ranging reflection. Education is not value-free: all students ought to be encouraged to confront questions of value.

Each volume examines both questions of approach and questions of content. Some contributors argue that an overtly Christian or religious framework for higher education actually affects the way we approach our study; a religious framework supports faith, while the secular framework is opposed to faith. Other contributors insist that a religious framework simply makes the curriculum wider. The approach will be the same as our secular counterparts; however, where the content of a course has a religious implication this will be included. Each volume brings out the diversity of positions held within the academy.

We have attracted the best writers to reflect on these questions. Each volume concludes by reflecting on the curriculum implications – the precise implications for educators in our schools and higher education colleges.

Ian Markham

The Contributors

The Revd Mark J. Cartledge is Chaplain and Tutor at St John's College, Durham.

Dr Bernadette Casey is Media Studies Subject Leader at the University College of St Mark and St John, Plymouth.

Dr Neil Casey is Senior Lecturer in Sociology at the University College of St Mark and St John, Plymouth.

Dr Sylvia Collins is Lecturer in the School of Social Sciences at Kingston University.

Dr Andrew Dawson is Lecturer in Theology and Religious Studies at University College, Chester.

Dr Colin Dawson is Sociology Subject Leader at the University College of St Mark and St John, Plymouth.

Ms Rosalind S. Fane is Research Assistant in the Centre for Theology and Education at Trinity College, Carmarthen.

The Revd Canon Professor Leslie J. Francis is D. J. James Professor of Pastoral Theology and Mansel Jones Fellow at Trinity College, Carmarthen, and University of Wales, Lampeter.

Dr Stephen J. Hunt is Lecturer in the Department of Sociology at the University of Reading.

The Revd Dr William K. Kay is Senior Research Fellow in the Centre for Theology and Education at Trinity College, Carmarthen.

The Revd Professor David Martin is Emeritus Professor of Sociology at the London School of Economics and Honorary Professor in the Department of Religious Studies at Lancaster University.

The Contributors

The Revd Canon Dr Martyn Percy is Director of the Lincoln Theological Institute, University of Sheffield.

The Revd Canon Professsor Ronald Preston is Emeritus Professor of Social and Pastoral Theology at the University of Manchester.

The Revd Philip Richter is Educational Development Officer at the Southern Theological Education and Training Scheme, based in Salisbury.

Ms Mandy Robbins is Junior Research Fellow in the Centre for Theology and Education at Trinity College, Carmarthen.

Mr Jeff Vass is Lecturer in Sociology in the School of Social and Political Studies at the University of Southampton, New College.

Dr Tony Walter is Reader in Sociology and Director of the MA in Death and Society at the University of Reading.

The Revd Canon Dr Michael West is Principal of the Local Ministry Scheme in the Diocese of St Edmundsbury and Ipswich.

The Revd Mandy Williams-Potter is Chaplain at Trinity College, Carmarthen.

Dr Andrew K. T. Yip is Senior Lecturer in the Department of Social Sciences at Nottingham Trent University.

Preface

Leslie J. Francis

C hristian universities and colleges have a unique opportunity to promote dialogue between theology and other
disciplines. The dialogue may emerge within the undergraduate
curriculum, within staff development, and within specific
emphasis in research. The Engaging the Curriculum initiative
has promoted this dialogue in a very specific way by sponsoring
consultations on the interface between theology and many of
the disciplines in which Christian universities and colleges have
an investment.

These consultations bring together individuals concerned
with the dialogue between theology and other disciplines from
the Anglican, Roman Catholic and Free Church colleges in
England and Wales, together with colleagues working in
secular colleges and universities. While Christian universities
and colleges make no claim to have a monopoly on such
dialogue, through the Engaging the Curriculum initiative they
have recognized and implemented their responsibility to
provide a forum through which such dialogue can be properly
recognized and progressed.

Part of this enquiry opens with a position paper by the Revd
Professor David Martin on how sociology might be pursued in
colleges with a Christian foundation. The Revd Canon
Professor Ronald Preston responds to Martin's presentation
from a theological perspective. Colleagues then respond to
these essays by illustrating how their current research interests
demonstrate the dialogue between theology and sociology in
practice. Two particular kinds of responses are offered.

The first kind of response focuses on *theoretical perspectives*
and illustrates how theology may contribute to an understanding of sociology or how sociology may contribute to an

understanding of theology. Examples of this kind of dialogue are presented in Part II through essays by Andrew Dawson, Rosalind S. Fane, Stephen J. Hunt, Martyn Percy, Jeff Vass and Tony Walter. These examples engage both with the broader issues of sociology as a discipline and with the specific concerns of the sociology of religion.

The second kind of response focuses on *empirical perspectives*, illustrating the kind of empirical research which might be undertaken by theologically informed and theologically motivated sociologists. Examples of this kind of dialogue are presented in Part III by Mark J. Cartledge, Bernadette Casey, Neil Casey and Colin Dawson, Sylvia Collins, Leslie J. Francis, William K. Kay, Philip Richter, Mandy Robbins, Michael West, Mandy Williams-Potter and Andrew K. T. Yip. These examples show sociology engaging with issues like glossolalia, the religiosity of young people, student motivation at a church college, church leaving, gay and lesbian Christians and local ministry. The sociological study of such issues cannot be properly pursued without theological awareness. At the same time, the church would be unwise to address such issues without taking a sociologically informed perspective into account.

All too often churches run the risk of undervaluing or ignoring sociological perspectives on matters of theological concern. At the same time, sociologists may run the risk of undervaluing the contribution which theology can make to their discipline. The present volume demonstrates just how much these two disciplines can engage in profitable collaboration both with Christian universities and colleges and within the wider academic community.

My work as editor of this collection of essays has been much helped by the patient and careful work of the contributors, and by the skill of my colleagues within the Centre for Theology and Education at Trinity College, Carmarthen, Diane Drayson, Ros Fane, Stephen Louden, Anne Rees and Mandy Robbins.

Leslie J. Francis
Trinity College, Carmarthen
September 1998

Part I Foundations

Christian Foundations, Sociological Fundamentals

David Martin

Introduction

T his essay is concerned with the problem of sociology and cognate subjects in colleges with a Christian foundation. That foundation might mean simply that such colleges tried to foster a different kind of community to that found elsewhere and set aside space for worship and for pastoral care. But in circumstances in which colleges are asked by government to reflect on their 'mission', meaning by that their fundamental purposes and objectives, the question arises as to whether the curriculum itself in its scope and tenor might take into account those purposes.

For reasons which will be set out below, any such question is fraught with problems when it comes to the human sciences. Whereas accountancy, for example, is presumably an unproblematic activity from the viewpoint of Christian foundations, the human sciences, and maybe sociology in particular, are far from unproblematic. They are, after all, angled disciplines, offering perspectives which include perspectives on religion. But over and beyond that, this problematic character is itself located in a tension between institutions of higher learning and religion deserving more sociological analysis. Thus, some distinguished American sociologists and historians recently engaged in elucidating the reasons why so many great institutions were founded with Christian intent, but are now identifiable as such only historically (such as Boston University) or by the retention of a name (such as Wesleyan University in Connecticut). Certainly in England the ordinary student will know nothing about the dissenting roots lying below the surface of such major institutions as Birmingham and Manchester universities.

With regard to sociology one needs also to take into account the historical genealogy of the discipline. In the United States sociology reproduced the national culture in its combination of the Enlightenment and the Christian Social Gospel, and in a weaker form one could locate parallel elements in Britain. In Europe, however, as its history and culture would lead one to expect, the genealogy bifurcates rather more sharply into the Enlightenment stem and a vigorous response, which was in part Catholic. But again, as with the origins of the universities, these complicated genealogies in the United States and Europe are well below the surface. Only historians of the subject know the extent of the roots of sociology in the Social Gospel, and the current stereotype of sociology is of a subject often taught from a political perspective and one whose basic assumptions are not easily reconciled with religious modes of understanding.

Nor is the stereotype entirely incorrect. If you were to go back to the mid-century you would find it amply illustrated. Students reading Barbara Wooton, for example, would have encountered the suggestion that Christians confronted with sociology would normally relinquish their faith. Certainly they would have had to be rather active and persistent in pursuit of intellectual support to the contrary, though such did exist, for example, in the work of J. Langmead Casserley (1951) and in the work of Catholic anthropologists and (somewhat later) in the approach of Edward Tiryakian (1962) or Jacques Ellul (1964). In any case, one aspect of the sociology of sociology was the contribution of Jews at the point of their emergence from the ghetto into a secular, even into a secularist, Enlightenment. There was an understandable edge discernible at that point in their treatment of religion which has now, for the most part, disappeared. Consider, for example, the tone and sympathetic vantage point of Daniel Levine (1992) in his *Popular Voices in Latin American Catholicism*.

The present moment is, therefore, interesting, since on the one hand some of the old hostilities have abated, and on the other hand the long-term tension between Christian institutional foundations and the content of academic work has emerged, yet again, in the context of what were often once teacher training colleges and are now of university status in their size and level of activity.

It goes without saying that there can be no attempt to revive a 'Christian' sociology, even though interesting work was once done under that head. Rather, I shall argue in what follows for an exploration of the full range of possible approaches within the rubric of independent and rigorous intellectual endeavour, given that some of these approaches are arguably compatible with religious understandings, or at any rate, with *some* religious understandings. Inevitably, there is a personal element here given that in this kind of discipline there are no absolutely mandatory paradigms apart from attention to logical inference, coherence and criteria of evidence. In a preliminary way one should always be wary of exclusive claims to the effect that only this or that mode of sociology is properly scientific. There is an extensive literature in the philosophy of science to rebut that particular kind of imperialism. For the rest, one might emulate Max Weber in seeing how much one can bear, and maybe also recollect what Herbert Butterfield (1957) had to say about being 'totally uncommitted' in the conclusion of his *Christianity and History*.

Language

Christianity is, among other things, a language and a mode of understanding. Some believe that language to be entirely self-contained, and if that is so, there can be no problems of negotiation over territories. But this is a costly solution which simultaneously restricts the range of Christianity and of other domains of human understanding and insight. Yet others believe there is a negotiation but one which is solely to the disadvantage of Christianity. Once the queen of sciences ruled and incorporated knowledge successfully into her wide empire, but each domain in turn acquired independence until the theological heartlands shrank to nothing. What the physical and biological sciences accomplished from the seventeenth century onwards, the social sciences completed from the eighteenth century onwards. The 'theological' mode was a

3

stage in historical development, and is no longer a power worthy of dialogue or negotiation since it has nothing left to offer. As it happens, this view is still residually present in contemporary sociological writing and more than residually present as an unexamined premise inside and outside sociology. It runs in parallel with the view that religion itself is a constantly shrinking power, doomed by social evolution to ghostly flittings at the margins of the real social world. That shrinking of religion would include its retreat in the university and in the 'Christian college', the very topic currently under review (see Marsden, 1990, 1994; Marsden and Longfield, 1993).

The two views just canvassed are that religion is safe within a bounded discourse, and that religion has undergone successive curtailments of power until it is inconsequential. These are contrary views. Both of them can show impressive intellectual pedigrees, distinguished proponents and significant power bases. They indicate immediately just how complicated are the relationships between Christian and sociological understandings, especially so if, as will be suggested later, there are essentially philosophical elements intervening in the negotiation and ensuring that sectors of argument are conducted on philosophical grounds.

Such contrary positions also indicate some of the sources of the sensitivities which surround the issue. Independence is an emotive matter, whether it is the postulated independence of theological discourse or the independence of work in the human sciences.

Without pursuing any further the two views just canvassed, it is at least clear that neither is compatible with a discussion of the forms a genuinely serious dialogue might take between religious and sociological understandings. Nor are they conducive to a discussion of what sensitivities might be cultivated and what issues probed by those who take seriously the Christian religion. This essay adopts a third view. The considerations here advanced presuppose that there is some possibility of fruitful dialogue between languages even if their scope and texture is different. But once that possibility is accepted it becomes clear that the character of the dialogue between sociology and theology differs considerably from the dialogue that might exist between theology and accountancy or law or physics. However briefly, we have now to sketch out *a distinctive* problem. Some zones of intellectual activity are relatively unproblematic for faith while others are problematic in very distinctive ways.

Amongst all the hundreds of books with titles based on some variant of 'Christianity and X' there can be few on Christianity and accountancy or Christianity and statistics or, extending the list, Christianity and engineering, numismatics, or horticulture. There are certain subjects which are concerned primarily with useful manipulations, or else are mostly descriptive in ways that appear quite neutral with respect to religious discourse. Other subjects, such as law and medicine, are almost equally neutral, apart from the moral issues to which they give rise, though in the case of medicine there is also a huge area of uncertainty with respect to the role of faith in, say, holistic therapies. There is a further group of subjects such as psychotherapy which raise questions of the relation between religious and secular terminologies, for example, whether or not the secular terminologies supersede the religious ones or extend them or emerge alongside them. Indeed, precisely this question of terminology emerges in sociology.

Before turning directly to sociology it is important to notice an important group of subjects, such as physics, cosmology, geology, palaeontology which have in the past raised questions about the biblical record. This frontier area is now quite well patrolled, apart from the recrudescence of such topics as 'creation science'. Much more frequent are eirenic discussions about design, order and beauty and elegance, related to the classical arguments for God's existence, in which scientists advance theological insights on their own account or claim to show some sort of consonance between religious and scientific concepts. These important discussions are assuredly not where the centres of contemporary turbulence lie. Somewhat more turbulence can arise with regard to modern developments in ethology, biology, genetics, behaviouristic psychology and brain science, particularly where these bear on human freedom or dignity or have implications for moral psychology. Even members of the general public are aware of the attacks launched by the biologist Richard Dawkins for whom religion itself can be characterized as a variety of virulent infection (see for example Dawkins, 1995; Bowker, 1995).

Whether the frontiers are silent or well-patrolled or subject to border-crossing or turbulence, the problems just mentioned are for the most part not of the same kind as those found in sociology, or in subjects deploying the same approaches as sociology, or in some way affianced to sociology in terms of humanistic method. The point about the deployment of sociological approaches is important, because while sociology is exposed to a great deal of vulgar and ignorant abuse as a pseudo-science or pseudo-subject, its perspectives have in fact infiltrated other cognate subjects to a remarkable degree. One may rephrase that by saying that sociology and these other subjects are porous. Setting aside the relationship between sociology and anthropology, which at the fundamental level is one of simple identity, there is a strong sociological element in politics and history as well as in educational studies and religious studies. So strong is this element that in a historian such as Keith Thomas it is built into his approach and, indeed, to his choice of subject matter, while in a historian such as Geoffrey Elton it elicits appeals against bowing down before the false gods of sociology. In the work of Fernand Braudel and others of the Annales School sociological understandings are an essential and entirely explicit layer in the overall texture of interpretation.

Whether these sociological understandings are generated from within sociology or have simply become one of the undisputed modes of 'modernity' (itself a much disputed sociological concept) hardly matters. There is a seepage in all directions, even at the level of terms, so that 'charismatic', for example, emerges in sociology and in politics from its original location in theology, and from thence it emerges again in everyday language. The word 'culture' is another instance. This means that those issues causing turbulence at the frontier of theology and sociology (or religion and sociology) are present along the whole frontier of the human sciences. They are, in short, intrinsic to *Geisteswissenschaften* and, thus, of signal importance. Indeed, they disturb subjects like English literature at least as much as subjects like sociology. Once the social context of literature is invoked, and once you are engaged in semiology and the interpretation of signs, it is not merely a question of difficult borders with theology but rather of all-round mutual penetration across borders between 'language' and 'society' and between language and science. Just how confused and contentious all that can become in terms of structuralism, post-modernism, etc. is well illustrated by the recent critique presented by Ernest Gellner (1992) in *Post-Modernism, Reason and Religion.*

Sociology, then, is as much a mode of understanding as a delimited subject. And just as that mode is present alongside others within other subjects, so a variety of modes are present within sociology. If such a characterization suggests there is no such entity as an essential sociology, the point is that there exists a recognizable cluster of approaches specifically intended to elucidate the web of social interactions considered as a whole. That cluster turns on the heuristic deployment of a *Homo sociologicus*, who is much closer to the 'whole' human being than *Homo economicus* and, therefore, exists at no great distance from *Homo theologicus* and all other fundamental understandings of the human, for example the philosophy of existentialism. The result is paradoxical. Once you have come that close to a holistic analysis you have to deploy different kinds of intention, different styles of elucidation, depending on the subject matter and the questions put to the subject matter. At one moment, for example, analysis may be synchronic, at another diachronic, and if it is the latter, then you are tracing connections over time and doing history. A sociologist analysing a ritual takes into consideration spatial arrangements and juxtapositions, the interpretation of texts, a complex choreography, and the dramatic shape of the liturgy. The point is that sociologists deploy many approaches. More than that, sociologists have at their disposal a variety of paradigms alongside the variety of approaches. Analyse any sociological text and it will yield root metaphors, implying, for example, organism or mechanism or theatre.

So holistic understanding requires many levels, many approaches, several paradigms, several root metaphors. Within this variety are some which are compatible with Christianity, others which are in tension with it, others perhaps even contrary to it. It is certainly not the business of a Christian college to select those which are compatible at the expense of those which are less so or at the expense of those which are clearly contrary. That is pre-emptive and inimical to the pursuit of truth. But arguably it *is* the business of a Christian college at least to allow some space and room for approaches which are compatible alongside those which are less so, unless and until they cease to generate fruitful results. Naturally, the notion of 'fruitful result' is difficult to apply, just as Lakatos' notion of a 'degenerating' research strategy is difficult to apply even in the physical sciences (Lakatos and Musgrave, 1970). It is a matter of judgement. In practice it is not all that difficult to discern a dead end and in sociology dead ends are quite few.

Two points are worth making at this juncture. One is that in the early stages of sociology many practitioners sought to devise a vocabulary which imparted an alien chill to the subject matter and so created an atmosphere of science. That phase of opaque technicality is by no means over, but it has become possible over the last few decades once more to use ordinary English. Subject matter can be less 'itself' when characterized in esoteric vocabularies than when characterized by all the resources of normal language. That is because sociology is by no means contrary to common sense in the way that the physical sciences are contrary. There was even a phase when some sociologists constantly surrounded ordinary concepts with inverted commas, in part to imply difficulty and in part to suggest esoteric special meanings. Now the inverted commas can be taken off again because in a very large number of instances there is no arcane otherness lurking beyond the ordinary. The contrived alienation of experience can be abandoned in favour of enhancement and enrichment. Permission to use English has once more been granted and should be exploited because the darkened glasses of esotericism did, indeed, convey an alienation of experience. Experience is not *systematically* false and a use of language which implies a special kind of scientific distance between experience and reality can itself be more of a falsification than it is an illumination.

The second point is this. Where metaphysics is concerned or maybe even where ethics is concerned, Christianity is often contrasted with humanism. That contrast is only marginally present in the human sciences because a Christian understanding of the human profoundly overlaps a humanistic or existentialist one. This is not to say that Christianity concedes 'Man is the measure of all things' but that it shares with humanism a view of what it is to be a human being in terms of meanings and purposes, and in terms of the existence and relevance of a 'life world' or *Lebenswelt*.

If human being is to be reduced by any of the numerous reductionisms on offer, then religious and humanistic under-standings stand or fall together. If, however, they stand together they can both deploy a common language and a language which is common in the cause of mutual enrichment. The extensions of understanding offered by imaginative literature are available for use over the whole range, provided there is also a rigorous deference to evidence. The flattened worlds of a restricted scientific intentionality necessary for specific purposes can be turned into an evocation of rounded worlds.

There is a further implication, now widely accepted, which is that the sociologist should at least show initial respect to the ways in which people recount their own experiences. Their stories are *prima facie* also evidence and what people say of themselves and their situation is not necessarily to be discounted. Such shifts in the scope of the sociological imagination should be placed before students for their consideration. Presumably, Christian teachers or a teacher in a Christian college would feel it potential enrichment to explore expanding permissions, even to expand them further where they did not contradict the fundamental rigours of evidence and inference. There could be no question of dogmatically commanding such extensions on the grounds that they were compatible with Christianity, but only a proper willingness not to refuse them dogmatically on the grounds that they were. And what could be more humanistic than that?

The above implies that sociology is close to literature, though not, of course, that it is itself a form of *belles lettres*. But what of its equally important proximity to history and how does that bear on the present concern? (This is an issue to be developed further in relation to the sociology of religion.)

The academic borders between sociology and history are, in my view, conventional and have turned classically on Dilthey's distinction between the ideographic and the nomothetic, or by way of a loose parallel, the particular and the general (Hodges, 1944). With only a little exaggeration, sociology seeks as much generalization as historical material can yield and that means that a sociologically minded historian is simply a member of that academic clan who has generalizing aspirations.

There are conventional demarcations as to topic, of course, and perhaps certain tell-tale modes of approach which mark out the historically-minded sociologist, such as a concern with milieux or with broad periodization, for example the issues raised by Bloch on feudalism, or the demarcation of a very wide-ranging process such as industrialization. Marxist historiography indifferently inhabits both sociology and history, and sociologists deploy the work of (say) Keith Thomas or Alan Macfarlane or Peter Burke or Peter Gay as easily as those historians deploy material from the social sciences and (in Gay's case) from psychoanalysis.

Narration

But there is a more important issue lurking here which bears more directly on present concerns, and it is the flow of events in time, and the irreducible role of narration. To take first the question of time, it is sometimes supposed that there is on the one hand a kind of political history obsessed with dates and maybe also with unfolding the national myth and its 'great men', and on the other hand a penetration of the holistic articulation of economic, cultural and demographic elements and the daily life of people such as characterizes the Annales school. Whatever particles of truth may be embedded in such a stereotype, the kind of history pursued by the Annales school is as firmly rooted in temporal succession as any other kind of history, quite apart from an ample recognition of the central role of power. Consider only what Braudel (1991) has to say about the ninth-century Treaty of Verdun. No serious comprehensive history can evade temporality. One might as well construct a crime novel without touching on the sequences of events and on what circumstances contributed in due course to what other consequences as construct a history without temporality and consequentiality.

The issue of temporality leads directly to the logic of narration. History turns on story and stories contain actors. The notion of 'actor' is central to contemporary sociology but it still needs to be emphasized that actors are particular people acting connectedly in time with motives and purposes as well as members of groups propelled by wider 'forces' in which they are entangled: droughts, plagues, economic innovations, migrations, new kinds of communication, the emergence of new types of weaponry and fighting force, and so on. There are in short innumerable particularities, and particular conjunctions both within patterns and actively shaping patterns, and among these particularities are active, distinctive, particular persons, not only a Lenin or a Mandela, who make a discernible and even a crucial difference, but also myriads of others who within every kind and degree of limiting circumstance construct their own biographies. As criminologists have observed, the criminal is both a creature of circumstance and a maker of a criminal career.

The point of such reflections is that it has sometimes in the past been possible to write sociology as if events and persons, and the narratives of events and persons, were externally powered by the 'motor' of constellations of power embodied in groups, classes or macro-formations. The real world, where the engines of both change and stability were located, constituted an impersonal realm dominated by unintended consequences. Thus, the logic of late capitalism decrees this or that and events and persons follow. It is no part of any sociologist's brief to extrude such 'logics' or the realm of unintended consequences, but a humanistic sociology also exists to include life worlds, particularities, events, persons and any number of possible stories. Indeed, many a sociological dialogue itself begins with the setting out of an intention to tell a particular kind of story and, of course, to see in the long run if stories link up or to some extent converge.

Now, religious understanding is based on the telling of a story, so much so that one contemporary brand of theology has even made 'story' a central category to the detriment of arguments and reasons and criteria. Judaism and Christianity (and perhaps to a lesser extent Islam) are narrations, constantly moving things on with sentences like 'And it came to pass'. Of course, 'salvation history' is not ordinary history, but it is an eventful narrative of the doings of individualized persons. A sociology which includes eventful narratives and persons purposefully active in their local circumstances and in their 'life worlds', and which also receives the 'testimony' of actors, is a sociology which does not radically alienate or separate the observer from the observed. By the same token, sociology receives the testimony of persons not only as data to be

David Martin

scrutinized and worked into an account at a different level concerned with formations, interests, logics and powers, but also in principle as a common human resource marking out a terrain shared by one person in fruitful *conversation* with another. Sociologists talk with people as well as about them.

It is perhaps worthwhile to indicate one version of humanistic sociology which not only concerns itself with events, particularities and persons in temporal sequence, but adopts as its root metaphor the notion of drama, scene, scenario, mask and role. In Victor Turner, for example, this is expounded in terms of transitional or liminal phases. In Irving Goffman it is expounded in terms of the presentation of self in everyday life. Among the original progenitors of the 'drama-turgical model' are such scholars as Kenneth Burke (1984). Clearly such a model of human action is continuous with a repertoire of models available in the more distant past and going back to the religious origins of drama itself. Such a continuity is yet another way of circumventing the contrived alienation of observer from observed insisted upon by dogmatic scientism.

Again, there is no suggestion that perspectives which alienate or distance observer from observed should not be tried and deployed. Equally there is no suggestion that the realm of unintended consequence or the mechanistic metaphor of 'motor' should be eschewed. It is important both to look on as a stranger and to participate as a fellow human. Much depends (and this is crucial) on whether the particular scientific intentionality involved in distancing and in the use of impersonal metaphors is a matter of ontological assertion, whereby the world is thus and only or merely thus, or simply a matter of trying all possible perspectives to see what they yield with respect to particular projects. The former is scientistic dogma, the latter retains the flexibility of science.

Reductionism

This distinction between substantive assertions as to how the world is and the tactical adoption of this or that perspective is crucial and it opens out on to a whole series of bruising controversies such as methodological individualism, whereby there are in the end only individuals, and reductionism, whereby there is, in the last analysis, only a given fundamental level of explanation. This is no place to enter upon such arcane disputes, but with regard to reductionism it should at least be noted that just as there exists a range of humanistic sociological perspectives so there exists a parallel range of humanistic psychologies and social psychologies which are, on the face of it, consonant with religious understandings. Contemplating the complete spectrum running from existential psychologies to socio-biological and behaviourist psychologies there seems to be a parallel spectrum running from the 'soft', inclusive, multitudinous, expansive, human-centred pole based on empathic understanding, to a more exclusive pole based on a few purportedly strong principles rooted in external explanation.

The psychology of B. F. Skinner, for example, constructed as it is in terms of stimulus and response, and particularly as expounded in *Beyond Freedom and Dignity* (Skinner, 1972) is presumably incompatible with Christian or humanist understandings. Even if Christianity were itself characterized as a form of determinism, with God hardening hearts and calling and predestining, the internal dynamics of God's sovereign providence would hardly be those articulated by B. F. Skinner. In a similar manner the 'hard' principles of needs and compensators as deployed by Rodney Stark (Stark and Bainbridge, 1985, 1987) in the explanation of religious phenomena do not easily jibe with religious understandings, at least if Stark's principles are assumed to be ontologically grounded and exhaustive. If psychologies constructed in terms of sub-personal models were combined with the impersonal models of sociology, it would be difficult to imagine how human beings ever imagined they were human. Alternatively, it is possible richly to combine a sociology which includes the human, with existentialist, phenomenological, interactionist and humanist psychologies which likewise yield humanly recognizable accounts. Typically they take the form of controlled and ordered insight, though they are inclined to strike those schooled in arts disciplines as extensions of the obvious. But in their application they can convert the obvious into the rich and surprising. At the most general level such psychologies are bound to be obvious as, for example, in G. H. Mead's (1934) account of the way personal identity is forged in encounters with the 'Generalized Other', but when it comes to rendering accounts of, for example, breakdowns or conversions, they enrich and expand understanding far beyond what unaided common sense might supply. For example, the kind of account of conversion yielded by the use of a psychologist such as Fingarette (1963) extends understanding without in any way reducing the experience of conversion itself or implying that those converted are puppets dangling on the strings of need or circumstance. On the contrary, converts can actively re-new, re-vise, re-cognize and re-organize their worlds.

If the autonomy of the human life world is to be accepted against reduction from the impersonal forces of society above and against reduction from the sub-personal forces below, then there ought also to be a parallel acceptance of culture as distinct from structure. Even some of those who in a broad way accept that sociology is a human science are inclined to conceive of structure as the nexus of origination and culture as derivative. So far as religion itself is concerned this view has run parallel to an emphasis on its removal as a structural principle (where it possesses at least the semblance of power by reason of being the guise of economics and politics) and its consignment to the status of one item in the hapless ensemble of mere cultural derivations. Of course, this is yet another variant of the dispute between ideal factors and material factors given that culture is understood as driven by the material 'base'. Once again the use of imagery and language is indicative in that the interwoven social skein is cut up into the real phenomena and the epiphenomena. To alter the imagery, factors emanating from the active core are viewed as pushing around the billiard balls of culture in a quasi-causal manner.

A contrary view, which needs at least to be articulated, would be that human creativity acts in complex concert with material elements, shaping them this way and that, reordering priorities, revising trajectories, modifying modes and reorganizing categories. Over time such creativity can undermine, or indeed shore up, the 'hard core' of social power, or else it may create a counter-culture, but it is emphatically not a passive recipient of impulses generated elsewhere. Such an approach would be based on the complementarity of culture and structure, ideal and material, understanding and explanation.

Relativity

If the issue just raised is one in which philosophical considerations are intimately involved the same is true of the issue of cultural relativity as it relates to moral relativity. Clearly the apparently widespread presumption of moral relativity must be a matter of some concern. It is widely suggested that value judgements made with respect to social practices and individual actions are undermined by the way such practices and actions are embedded in, enmeshed in and, therefore *relative* to, a social context. Now it is, of course, obvious that practices and actions occur in context and it is part of the sociological task to elucidate that context. What, however, remains not at all obvious is the postulated connection between the existence of a context for actions and the refusal morally to evaluate such actions. Supposing, for example, that suttee or female infibulation were shown in some way to be meshed in with other social practices: no moral guidance could logically emerge as to whether widows should expire on the funeral pyres of their husbands or young girls suffer infibulation. Again, it is doubtless the case that whaling is part of the culture of particular regions of Norway and Japan but this in itself hardly destroys the moral judgements which bear on whether or not whaling is supportable. Contexts and judgements mix, and inform each other, but the existence of contexts does not reduce judgements to mere emotivity. This is precisely the kind of argument lying behind a moral relativism which appeals to cultural relativity. Moreover, exactly the same type of argument is involved in the move from observation of the fact of moral pluralism in Western society, whereby we differ in some of our values, to a conclusion about the impropriety of evaluating one moral judgement above another or, indeed, one culture above another. It is one thing to sensitize young people to the contexts in which people in other countries or in other times act differently from ourselves. That serves to secure a suitable pause for reflection rather than instant evaluation. It is quite another thing, however, to suggest that every practice is equally worthy of respect.

In fact, contrary to what many suppose, the effect of sociology (or rather the effect of the motivation for doing the subject) is often not moral relativity but hyper-moralism. This hyper-moralism is directed from the vantage point of our Western liberal present against most human (and inhuman) practice elsewhere. Whereas on the one side there is seeming tolerance for a teeming variety of cultures and personal behaviour, there is also a tendency to judge cultures in terms of utopian perspectives and in particular to evade the ineluctable bases of human society and group relations in structures of authority and violence. This is virtually a religious rejection of the world emerging in sociological form. To recount the structural conditions constraining contemporary events in the Balkans is to invite something approaching moral incredulity, even offence.

So, sometimes, the problem is less a refusal of moral judgement so much as an immediate rush to judgement against whatever does not conform to the strictest exemplification of Franciscan or ecological ideals. To convey to students the *realpolitik* in which international relations are universally grounded is to invite suspicion of personal cynicism, even though such understanding is entirely compatible with a politically radical analysis and can easily emerge from such an analysis. So, while on the one hand individual and personal virtue can be viewed externally as generated by 'system needs' or, at any rate, driven rather than chosen and culpable, whole systems can be roundly condemned as morally tainted or, if one cares to put it so, implicated in 'structural sin'. In my personal view, they *are* so implicated but our judgements on them need to be somewhat reserved and cautious in relation to time and place, as well as in relation to the universality of evil. In other words, a sociotheological problem arises in the context of utopian thought as counterposed to original sin. However, this ought not to be pursued in sociology itself but in some other more appropriate context. Where, then, is the appropriate place?

The options with regard to moral perspective are happily not restricted to an antinomian relativism and a utopian rush to judgement. There is an open space to be cleared somewhere for serious moral debate on personal behaviour, social conditions and their interconnection. In my own view, this debate could engage many of our students and needs to be pursued way beyond some preliminary introduction to the distinction between fact and value or, indeed, the kind of semi-empirical accounts of moral development found in Jean Piaget and Lawrence Kohlberg. Students of the human sciences who are being introduced to the tangled skein of social connectedness and historical consequentiality, would benefit above all by some introduction to classical moral reflection. Without an informed insight into the making of moral judgement in relation to the consequences of policy, intended and unintended, and the dynamics of cultural life, they become mere practitioners.

Could this be the right space for a contribution which includes the moral perspectives of the faith communities of this country? After all, those perspectives have historically provided the 'Great Codes' which bound whole civilizations together and made them distinctive. Moreover, this is the space where views of 'the human' embodied in philosophical anthropology have their special purchasing power.

Clearly two conditions would be important. One is that moral reflection can come from any angle whatsoever. The other is that there is strong emphasis on the cultural and historical context of moral judgement. Students could become so bemused by, say, the complexities of Kant's categorical imperative that they never tested out judgements against the realities of cultural conditions and social circumstances.

From what kind of sources could a Christian contribution come? Dorothy Emmet (Emmet and MacIntyre, 1970) and Basil Mitchell (1980, 1994) have both written with a strong awareness of social context. Alasdair MacIntyre's *After Virtue* (1981) and *Whose Justice? Which Rationality?* (1988) offer an introduction to a postulated moral breakdown of the 'Enlightenment Project'. In Stanley Hauerwas (1988), there is a truly vital debate about contemporary issues likely to stir up the most torpid. Indeed, in the United States, one can encounter a constant and high-level debate involving such people as Robert Bellah, Gregory Baum, Peter Berger, Richard Neuhaus, Paul Ramsey, Max Stackhouse, Robert Benne and others, which could stimulate students to think about their own society. In Britain there are important contributions to be tapped in, amongst others, John Habgood, Jonathan Sacks, Mary Warnock, Robin Gill, Duncan Forrester, A. H. Halsey and Charles Elliott. The kind of material that feeds this debate can be located, for example, in Ian Markham's (1994) *Plurality and*

Christian Ethics, concerned with civic culture, problems of truth in relation to tolerance, the scope of the state and intermediary associations like church, synagogue, temple and mosque.

Summing up, the nub of the argument has been to suggest that Christian colleges and teachers with some Christian concern might consider how far students are exposed to the full range of approaches, and how far the language and metaphors we use imply mechanism and reduction of the 'human' to other levels of analysis in terms of superhuman forces or biological needs and programmes. The human sciences allow a wide range of kinds of scientific intentionality and the problems of the human sciences respond to a variety of approaches. Many of these are humanistic and interpretative in that they do not require an alien language distancing the observer from the observed but rather require a common language of rigorous scrutiny and interpretation. The human sciences are Janus-faced, with one face turned to the hermeneutic or interpretative sciences and, therefore, susceptible to many kinds of frame and allowing many kinds of story to be told. There is a further case for hinting at the need for some sociological humility before the impenetrable skein of interaction, such as is recommended, for example, in the work of von Hayek (1967). Academics are allowed to shock by suggesting such people at least be read.

Insofar as active humans inhabit a life world and mould their circumstances in an eventful narrative, there is a consonance with religious understandings which should be allowed a place in academic exposition alongside approaches less consonant. By the same token, the philosophical elements in the practice and maybe the substance of sociology itself should not be submerged but actively brought to the surface for inspection, in particular those elements which derive from a philosophy of history or an ideology of progress, or which divide up the social too easily into the efficacious and the narrative. It is not a matter of extrapolating from religious dogma to a particular version of sociology held to fit with that dogma, but of allowing the full range of approaches to be exhibited, including those which happen to be consonant with religious understanding and which do not violate the agreed canons for ensuring truthful outcomes.

Sociology of religion

Arguably, the manner in which the Christian colleges handle the social sciences of religion, including the sociology of religion, is at the heart of any question about what makes them distinctive. Equally arguably nothing turns on such matters at all. Knowledge is knowledge and that is all there is to be said. Does the religious foundation of New College, Oxford imply anything about the way its Fellows teach Economics? Surely not. What follows here has to be an exploration into unknown territory to see what, if anything, is there by someone who has spent most of an academic life in the entirely secular world of the London School of Economics and Political Science. I can only offer reflections for debate. Perhaps those who consider it starts off from a non-existent question might read it as an essay on the state of the subject as I see it.

This is not a bad moment, so far as the subject is concerned, to clarify and reconsider, given that there has been a partial gap in recruitment and that a younger generation has now emerged. Two elements are bound to be central, one to do with the guiding presuppositions of the subject, the other to do with the range of topics selected for coverage. Clearly, the two will be linked since presuppositions do affect what is accounted central and what accounted peripheral. To place queries against the one is to place queries against the other. Placing queries of this kind in no way implies that the standard curriculum of the subject since the 1960s is unimportant or other than richly instructive. It is, after all, perfectly possible to write a classic on the Mennonites of France which irrigates our whole field of study. Clearly there exists a distinguished body of work, much of it cited all over the English-speaking world, which deals, for example, with sects, secularization, millenialism, new religious movements, religion in the United States, or the new religious Right, to say nothing of commentaries on the classics. One thinks of scholars of the stature of Bryan Wilson or Mary Douglas in the senior British generation, or of such distinguished people as Robert Wuthnow (1989) among somewhat younger scholars in the United States. If the staple diet is not much canvassed in this essay, that is because some things can be taken as read. This is not a bibliographical survey of settled terrain. At the same time, our own worlds and the worlds beyond our shores are changing very fast. As Roland Robertson (1978, 1992) and others have stressed for some years, we are immersed in a global situation in which new themes engage our attention and dramatic developments force us to stand back and think again. Presumably, if students are our focus of concern, it is important not only for them to have a good idea of what has gone on in the academic world of the sociology of religion, but also to understand what is going on in the world itself, particularly as that involves religion. It is a moot point whether the subject as practised provides much by way of access to, say, the major developments in the Middle East or in Africa. I would imagine there are ways of finding such things out, but our foci of concern rarely push us to pursue them (Gifford, 1998).

The omission of much of the human race is not necessarily culpable. Writing as one benevolently thrust into the epochal changes in contemporary Latin America, I can testify to the restriction of vision which can come about in the course of teaching, and even to the restrictive power of the governing paradigms. Indeed, the epochal events concerned were well-nigh forbidden by the paradigm, and if they were not forbidden, their recognition was seriously occluded. Forty million Latin Americans just could not have been converted to a genuinely indigenous version of Pentecostal and evangelical faith (Martin, 1990).

If we pause to listen to our own unguarded professional discourse in the ordinary flow of academic conversation there is a world of assumption there, simultaneously easing the flow of ideas and also damming it up. The lens constricts. There is, in short, a sociology of our knowledge as English-speaking sociologists of religion, as well as a contingent history of the subject, including our personal biographies, affecting the direction and distribution of our concerns.

Pausing for a moment on this particular issue, we can probably admit that many topics central to the issue of religion in the world at large lie at the edge of our vision but directly in the sights of other disciplines. Scholars such as Bryan Turner (1983), Steve Bruce (1992) and James Beckford (1989) have sought in different ways to extend our coverage, but if what interests us is religion, whenever and wherever it occurs, then we have to co-opt academic neighbours in history, political science, race relations, area studies, social geography, religious studies and international affairs. This is not simply because collectively they are many and we are few or because they are already cryptosociologists. The point is that they are the ones who do those kinds of thing, perhaps because they carry on their intellectual lives on the basis of different presuppositions. Suppose we take an innovative study like *Confession* by Turner and Hepworth (1982), we find its intellectual resources are elsewhere in studies of deviance.

A massive challenge to our understanding might, in my view, emerge were we to take on board a mass of material across disciplines which takes in mainstream events in a global perspective. Included in that would be the challenge to our understanding, indeed our human comprehension, posed by Rwanda and Bosnia. Once in the academic mainstream and fully seized of a global perspective, our crucial materials would include journals like *Africa* or *The Journal of Church and State* or *Cross Currents* or any one of a dozen others.

If one wanted examples of what has not so far lain in the foreground of our interest, one might consider the contribution of Catholicism and Catholic thinking to postwar, European reconstruction and to the eventual breakdown of the division of Europe. There is a history here from Adenauer, Monnet, De Gaulle and Schuman to Delors which is of the utmost importance and which has even brought the word 'subsidiarity' into our own political parlance. What do we know of the contributions of Catholic family policy to the Social Chapter? Yet the ascendancy and now the crisis of Christian Democracy has remained someone else's field of study. The same is true of the role of Poland, a Polish Pope and Polish Catholicism in bringing down the Russian empire. Do we consider and recommend the work of Timothy Garton Ash or Mark Almond (cf. Casanova, 1994)? These are *the* events of our own day, yet it is a question as to how far they disturb or alter what we teach. How have the paradigms and intellectual genealogies kept us in place when we could, in fact, face on to the world?

Insider knowledge and outer indices

At this point we need to back up somewhat to raise again the issues of the fundamental approaches discussed earlier in the consideration of sociology as such, and to rework them a little for more specific purposes. In due course, those issues will lead back again to the selection of topics. The important point is that they are at the axes of the human sciences. They cannot be avoided and admit of no neat solution.

Fundamentally there is a dialogue, and occasionally an excommunication, between several variants of explanation in the sense of 'because of' and several variants of understanding (in the sense of 'in order to'). There are positivistic accounts concentrating on ascertainable externals and there are humanistic and interpretative accounts focused on meaning. Thus, to give an example, there are statistical series for baptisms over long periods of time, and there is the question of what baptism means (in terms, for example, of resurrection after a death by water) and of what people themselves suppose it to mean (in terms, for example, of entry into the community or a prophylactic against disease). It is self-evident that the sociology of religion requires both in order to be pursued at all.

However, the main problems lie somewhat athwart this division, important though it is, and they have to do with reductionism. There are reductionist tendencies within positivism which denature religion to reveal a more powerful explanatory layer, but there are also reductionist tendencies within interpretative sociologies which radically decode religious language in terms of other discourses.

Not even a major article devoted solely to these issues could unravel the crosscutting complexities lurking in them, particularly given the different meanings accorded to positivism and to humanism. Much depends on how exclusive are the claims of a particular approach and whether an ontological assertion is involved rather than a methodological tactic for delimited analytic objectives. The underlying point, however, is quite simple. If religion is only the surface outcrop of a more fundamental layer, or if religion is subject in principle to radical decomposition, then the status of *any* religious discourse is totally undermined.

It is *not* necessary to maintain that everything is as it seems or to argue that discourses are sealed off in the Winchian manner, but it *is* necessary to reject radical and systematic reductions and decompositions. It so happens that few in the discipline pursue these radical courses, though the language of needs and compensations used by Rodney Stark, for example, seem to point in that direction. The problem is rather to note a glib and uncontrolled deployment of partial decompositions in an *ad hoc* manner: a touch of psychoanalysis, a hint of sociobiology, an implication suggesting pathology. As I. M. Lewis (1976) once commented in relation to anthropology: the discipline 'lives in sin' with psychoanalysis.

Excluding radical decompositions which must surely be anti-religious in implication, it is interesting that the positions taken up within the discipline probably do not correlate all that closely with personal attitudes to religion or to politics. At most there is a concentration of religiously sympathetic scholars engaged in the elaboration and extension of interpretative approaches. An example of this cross-bench situation would be C. Wright Mills, who at one stage was a key figure in the general sociological debate. Mills was a political radical and non-believer who in his *The Sociological Imagination* (1959) attacked what he called the 'abstracted empiricism' of Talcott Parsons, who was (if I understood him rightly) a Christian or, at least, highly sympathetic.

In the earlier discussion of general sociology it was suggested that interpretative, 'dramatistic', and phenomenological socio-logies were, on the face of it, consonant with religious understandings. Certainly, the sociology of religion contains distinguished exponents of such sociologies. Perhaps the best-known names are Peter Berger, Thomas Luckmann, Clifford Geertz and Victor Turner. Berger and Luckman have developed phenomenological understandings (Berger and Luckmann, 1966; Luckmann, 1967; Berger, 1969), drawing particular instruction from the analyses of the 'life-world' by Alfred Schutz. Berger is the sociologist most cited in the discipline and a seminal influence. Clifford Geertz is another seminal influence who has taken further the 'dramatistic' kind of analysis pioneered by Kenneth Burke. Geertz, who is, perhaps significantly, an anthropologist, crosses disciplinary bound-aries, points up the convergence of theories in a variety of fields, and encourages a non-scientist understanding of culture. Victor Turner, another anthropologist, also worked across disciplines, and a good statement of his position is found in *Dramas, Fields and Metaphors: Symbolic Action in Human Society* (Turner, 1974).

David Martin

Interpretation and meaning

The argument is, then, that a given range of sociologies of religion is not inherently hostile in terms of social ontology to religious modes of understanding. Furthermore, this range arises from the nature of the subject and certainly not by extrapolation from religious positions. Indeed, extrapolation of that kind would be intolerable and impossible. Presumably these sociologies can and should be fully canvassed and explored in Christian colleges alongside all others. It would be paradoxical were the reverse true. There is, however, a further point to be made. If such sociologies should *not* be acceptable as an agreed part of what is on offer, then the whole of the humanistic sector of the university disappears at the same time. The humane and human world as we understand it is phantasmagoria. Such an extreme conclusion cannot *a priori* be excluded and, indeed, some psychologies do proceed as if the inner world of our experience were epiphenomenal. But sociology, including the sociology of religion, is tilted strongly in the reverse direction, and much of the abuse it receives about not being a science arises precisely from this humane orientation and from its openness to what is (in the profound meaning of the word) 'common sense'. This essay, at any rate, rejects radical reductionism and assumes the existence of emergent properties at higher levels of organization. Language alters all. From this point on, therefore, it argues that the sociology of religion, to be most productive, is properly linked to other disciplines in the humanities based on the same humane premiss; and in due course it will further argue that the two disciplines which maximize that productivity are history and politics. But that argument itself requires a prior examination of the discipline of meaning itself, that is, hermeneutics.

The sociology of religion is a hermeneutic discipline and, arguably, a sociologist of religion has to grapple with the hermeneutic problem, and maybe with its principal exponents. Certainly one cannot in practice evade principles of interpretation. This creates fruitful openings on to the literary critical field and on to the study of sacred texts, including the Bible. There is a lot to be said for exposure to texts and testimony. Those who have done this, even with unlikely material, have found themselves engaged in an unexpected way. Bernice Martin (1981), for example, sought understanding as well as eliciting it, in the study of religious themes in the rock lyric. If T. E. Hulme (1960) was right and there is something called 'split religion', or something very like it called by Edward Bailey (1997) 'implicit religion', then we need to be skilled in uncovering trace marks and recognizing fragments of themes. Students could be introduced rather more than they are to the thematic repertoire of religion and that might well engage with their own prehensile explorations. They are often both very ignorant and oddly experienced in these matters. Too often we (and I include myself) offer them a vocabulary to do with objects of study rather than saying 'Listen to this' or 'What do you make of that?' That would be the beginning of hermeneutics.

Perhaps the best-known names in the field of hermeneutics are Paul Ricoeur and Hans-Georg Gadamer. It is a great pity we do not have an accessible study of them both to provide a prolegomenon to the sociology of religion. Ricoeur (1976) makes two points important for present concerns. He writes of a 'hermeneutic of appropriation' as well as a 'hermeneutic of suspicion', and he recommends 'conversation'. Suspicion cannot be relaxed, of course. Whatever the dangers of radically reductionist decoding, one must 'read into' texts and testimony what is not in the surface presentation. There *are* deflections: an open discourse about life may be a secret discourse about death. Yet alongside suspicion there is this necessary 'hermeneutic of appropriation' which partakes of the nature of a conversation.

Those teachers who take students to a Hare Krishna ceremony or even traditional Evensong have initiated a conversation. The sociology of religion concerns what George Herbert called 'something understood' which comes through all the senses as well as the intelligence. Of course, there are other hidden agendas to be probed, elicited and (in the proper sense of the word) exposed. But we need also to allow the face-to-face equality of a conversation.

Above all in Ricoeur one is reminded of the polyvalent potency of sign, symbol and image. Sunk inside the sign is a vast realm of possibilities brought to light in differing ways according to context and occasion, but also swimming up towards the surface under close inspection. Religions are languages of the body and they unveil themselves in gesture or disposition of limbs. Some students have only rarely seen the body disposed in that particular way, for example, as massed in Muslim observance. Nor have they properly imagined the lighting of a candle in Christian prayer. What does it mean to teach about certain ascertainable externals within our sub-discipline when the phenomenon is not offered for apprehension as a language? Why would a lecture on just one item in that language, like lighting a candle, be so unusual, even perhaps so professionally dangerous an innovation? Candles are lit to John Lennon, the late King of Norway, the Virgin Mary and Princess Diana (Walter, 1999). In the relevant lexicon a candle is light, enlightenment, reason, remembrance, thanks, respect, continuity, resurrection. A hermeneutic of appropriation requires this as prior knowledge. Can we begin to explain what we have simply just not understood? This is not a matter of abandoning a hard-nosed scepticism but of questioning our prejudgements.

The emphases of Hans-Georg Gadamer point in the same direction. Readers and texts are engaged in mutual dialogue which allows the readers to go out to other worlds before returning to their own. That involves a conversation with the past and (a point to be developed below) with everything involved in tradition, that is, in retention, memory and continuity.

Extending the range

The prior importance of hermeneutics, if accepted, extends the range of the subject and its subject matter. Once one has secured entry into the endlessly refracted and refractory realm of meanings, the interior of the subject is thrown open for exploration. Permissions are given instead of warning notices, and openings are offered instead of restrictive practices. These permissions and openings are very important, provided (and this is crucial) they are not used as indulgences. Academics, let alone students, are surprisingly deferential when it comes to the permissions of their peers about what is and what is not available territory.

No doubt anthropologists have long had a different map of permissions and restrictions. If all this is wrong about the sociology of religion, then I am sorry in more ways than one, because I have myself intuited non-existent inhibitions and obeyed an inward fear not an outer norm. Three examples occur to me, now distant enough in time to be referred to. They reinforce the sense that there has been a restrictive norm and that I have been rightly fearful.

The first example goes back twenty years, when I was engaged with others in a discussion of David Starkey's (1978) marvellously innovative study of body symbolism and the significance of degrees of personal intimacy at the Tudor Court. The Privy Council and the Groom of the Stool were keys to unlock the inner workings both of religion and power. This was an intimate introduction to the powers of the sacred and the dreadful sanctities of power. Hostility from the assorted social 'scientists' was patent and I was pushed to mount a defence of the work in terms which included the propriety of the subject matter.

The second example refers to the inaugural lecture of the late Maurice Freedman in which he offered a delicate analysis of the whole course of a Chinese wedding. No one could accuse Freedman of being other than very toughminded, but in permitting himself such a subject he was, literally, exposing what some thought should not be exposed, even in anthropology. One very distinguished colleague commented 'Why did he choose to expose himself with so feminine a topic before all our colleagues?' Could it even be then that our self-definition is affected by some need for trenchant masculinity?

The third example is somewhat more recent and concerned the topic of sacrifice. It was suggested that anthropologists and sociologists meet with one or two properly certificated theologians (for example, the then Professor Stephen Sykes) to discuss sacrifice. I can only record a *frisson* of unease and something beyond a mere hermeneutic of suspicion. Here was a topic dangerously close to the heart of religion, pathological or otherwise, and it was to be talked about with theologians. I did not myself attend the discussion but the results are to be found in a rather neglected volume *Sacrifice*, edited by Fortes and Bourdillon (1980).

The problem was clear and I suspect it would remain clear even to a younger scholarly generation. This cross-disciplinary initiative extended boundaries in a way that could compromise academic identities. In short we, of all people, were afraid, checked by problems of identity which we, of all people, were trained to understand and circumvent. No doubt the anthropologists carried the thing off because the subject matter was mostly located outside traditions in our own vicinity. That would be my point. Anthropologists have acquired such freedoms more easily than sociologists because they are principally exercised in relation to the Lugbara and the Nuer. But even among anthropologists there has been the shadow of inhibition. As recently as the early 1970s, Raymond Firth (1973, p. 162) wrote about a recovery of interest in symbols in and for themselves and not merely as surrogates for and evasions of the real. So far as the sociology of religion is concerned, more particularly in what we deliver to students, I suspect the matter has been only indifferently reformed.

But what *kind* of topic could be brought from the periphery to the centre were we more fully to explore the permissions now on offer? A major example would be the nature of tradition. Tradition, after all, has to do with the conservation of meanings and is crucial for general sociology, let alone the sociology of religion. There is absolutely no reason why its analysis should be confined to those with conservative agendas. The meanings may be established or dissident or whatever, but they are stored, protected, handed on, revised, attenuated, renewed, recovered. The whole enterprise of oral history and history from below had to do with the salvage of traditions, as did E. P. Thompson's (1968) *The Making of the English Working Class*. The sociology of tradition is central to all kinds of major debates, whether we consider the conflict between modernizers and traditionalists in the churches or in the political parties. How does the sacred protect banked-up resources? How are traditions reinvented as, for example, traditions of monarchy were reinvented by the Edwardians? Nevertheless, in spite of all this richness, how far is the topic of tradition remembered in the construction of our bibliographies? And to what resources might we have recourse? A difficult but relevant example would be R. K. Fenn's (1992) *The Death of Herod*.

To my own limited and unaided recollection one might have recourse to the following. My first example illustrates the basic point rather too well since virtually no one now remembers the seminal work of Maurice Halbwachs, *Les Cadres Sociaux de la Mémoire* (Halbwachs, 1976) and *La Mémoire Collective* (Halbwachs, 1950). Edward Shils' (1981) magisterial volume *Tradition* makes the basic point differently: 'Tradition is a dimension of social structure which is lost or hidden by the atemporal conceptions which now prevail in the social sciences' (Shils, 1981, p. 7). The point is well taken.

What else then on tradition? There is Karl Mannheim's (1952) essays on conservative thought and the problem of generations, S. N. Eisenstadt's *From Generation to Generation* (Eisenstadt, 1956) and *Tradition, Change and Modernity* (1973) and P. Connerton's (1989) *How Societies Remember*. There is also Daniéle Hervieu-Léger's *La Religion pour Mémoire* (1993) about communities of memory, and *Vers un Nouveau Christianisme* (1986). Active bibliographical exploration could no doubt uncover more, such as Jack Wertheimer's (1992) *The Uses of Tradition: Jewish Continuity in the Modern Era*, or Menachem Friedman's (Friedman and Heilman, 1994) studies of the cultural reproduction of ultra-orthodox Jewry. And the list could be extended by including themes from a much older layer of sociology on related topics like custom, habit, folkways and mores. But it is clear how exigent is our concern, and how little note we in general take of tradition in our own Western society even though a postmodern perspective may well return us to questions of time and memory. Tradition is past, it is elsewhere and it is residual. For the most part, we focus rather on its passing, as in Paul Heelas' excellent work on detraditionalization (Heelas, Lash and Morris, 1995) or, a generation back, Daniel Lerner's (1958) *The Passing of Traditional Society*.

One or two other volumes recently published are worth a mention because they serve to indicate the lacunae to be filled, and significantly link up with the theme of tradition. The volume edited by Jon Davies and Isabel Wollaston (1993), *The Sociology of Sacred Texts*, includes a major section on the commemoration of death, either in war memorials or in the holocaust. Another volume edited by M. Sallnow and J. Eade (1991) is entitled *Contesting the Sacred: The Anthropology of Christian Pilgrimage*. This latter volume explores a theme opened up by Victor Turner but it is still a theme able to benefit from a great deal more amplification. Tens of millions of our fellow Europeans go on pilgrimage to Lourdes or Zaragoza, Knock or Santiago, the Normandy beaches or Rocamadour, Auschwitz or Jerusalem. The modern interpenetration of pilgrimage and tourism is as interesting as the medieval interpenetration of pilgrimage and economic activity. The postmodern enters in here once more in relation to the consumption of tradition as sign, symbol and artefact.

Secularization: some disadvantages?

At this juncture one has inevitably to discuss some disadvantages of having secularization as a crucial problematic in the sociology of religion. It does, after all, involve the demise or marginalization of religion and fits into major hypotheses about processes determining *the* future of modern society, notably rationalization as propounded by Max Weber and his successors. The particular disadvantages canvassed here also link with earlier comments about atemporality and an inadequate exploration of meaning, and they will connect later with comments about the paramount need for sociology to be affianced to history, including times, places, narratives and persons. It is worth saying that the disadvantages mentioned are not so much logically required by the nature of the problematic, as contingently likely. Let us call them the associated tendencies of theories of secularization. That is true, for example, of the first disadvantages to be discussed: the scanting of meaning. How might that come about? Maybe in the following way.

If rationalization is, indeed, pursuing a majestic progress towards universal secularity, then the particular and varied substantive meanings it obliterates can seem of rather secondary importance. Why enter into the last rites of a dying world, except for nostalgic or antiquarian reasons? If mainstream religion is becoming marginal and even more if it is literally inconsequential, then the interest in epiphenomenal margins need not be all that great.

One may add in relation to this scanting of meaning that the presentation of data on secularization has tended to have a quasi-objective character, whatever the particular thrust of the argument. Quite properly there is much citation of statistics on church attendance, rites of passage, private prayer, patterns of belief, proportions of published books devoted to religious themes, even proportions of GNP devoted to religious purposes. Matters become uncomfortably complex, however, if one feeds into this debate changing meanings within the rite, though there is admittedly some citation of attitudinal studies concerning shifting conceptualizations of God. Nevertheless, this complexity is central and not adequately canvassed.

There is a deeper problem here which cross-cuts the problematic of secularization, though it is well illustrated by the way secularization is handled. That problem concerns the precarious and difficult link between the data and the processes as outlined by sociologists and the mutation of cultural meanings and of ideas as dealt with by cultural historians. Thus, the magisterial study by Owen Chadwick (1975) of *The Secularization of the European Mind in the Nineteenth Century* is split between a rather incidental chapter on sociological indices and the fundamental argument to do with ideas and meanings. My *A General Theory of Secularization* (1978) is split in the reverse direction. R. K. Webb's (1980) query about where that work would or could fit in the growth (and decline?) of Unitarianism into its argument underlines the problem. Unitarianism is part of a major shift of ideas, presumably in a secular direction, particularly in the United States, but sociologists pay little attention to it, and are perhaps not certain how such attention could be paid. A reinforcing instance could be provided by the problem of incorporating some crucial shifts in, say, the ideological field between 1890 and 1914. Changes in the Edwardian era analysed by such scholars as Jonathan Rose (1986) and Samuel Hynes (1968) are of enormous relevance to the issue of secularization. But so long as sociological theory processes history and ideas, the worlds of cultural history and sociology of religion will stay too far apart. Of course, the polar opposite of high-level sociology is simply to write history as if it were a reflection of philosophy or ideas. Some of Don Cupitt's views appear to be framed on precisely such premises.

Another major tendency associated with the problematic of secularization is the plausible link between the setting forth of the process of marginalization and a concentration on sects and new religious movements. Clearly, the study of sects is immensely rewarding as is evident in the work of Bryan

Wilson, Lantenari, O'Dea and many others. Equally the same is true of new religious movements as is evident in the work of Paul Heelas, Eileen Barker, James Beckford, Roy Wallis, Anson Shupe, David Bromley and others. Such movements may well be harbingers of new spiritualities and a new eclecticism burgeoning in younger generations.

But the weight of contribution here does have consequences, for example, in the teaching of religious aspects of the sociology of modern Britain as well as in the sociology of religion itself. All too often the teaching of modern Britain proceeds by initially despatching the mainstream bodies under the head of statistical declines. There follows a brief aside on non-Christian religions essentially under the head of ethnicity, before turning to issues to do with sects and new religious movements. Internal shifts of great moment within mainstream religion are rarely considered in depth, unless maybe when tagged to some issue like gender. There are some undergraduate texts extant which evacuate the topic of religion altogether.

Things are happily altering and have been further amended with the publication of Grace Davie's (1994) *Religion in Britain since 1945*. There are important contributions on politics and religion by George Moyser and Kenneth Medhurst (1988), and there are also very useful compendia edited by Paul Badham (1987) and Terence Thomas (1988), though these contributions are again mostly from outside the discipline. What we lack, for example, is any sense of the complex web of relationships between region, religion and politics which was brought to view in the wake of John Smith's death. One might ask just why so many of Labour's recent leaders come from nurseries in the culture of the peripheries or in the culture of religious dissent, or from both together? But these are cultures about which we know very little from the perspectives of the sociology of religion. It would almost be true to say that the larger the institution the smaller the attention paid to it.

A third tendency associated with secularization theory is a smoothing out of the historical record with the result that historians have to render adequately complex what has been initially over-simplified. For example, Jon Butler's (1990) *Awash in a Sea of Faith*, together with varied contributions by Rodney Stark and Roger Finke (1986), showed that churchgoing and modernity in the United States were positively associated from 1800 to 1950. Whatever that may say about secularization in the long run, it necessitates a major revision of the inner dynamics of secularization as hitherto specified, and it also raises a question about European exceptionalism as an alternative to American exceptionalism. Is Europe 'out of step', not America and the rest of the world? An excellent debate about the issues involved here is available in *Religion and Modernization*, edited by Steve Bruce (1992), with contributions from Hugh McLeod, Robin Gill, Callum Brown, Roger Finke, Steve Bruce, Roy Wallis and Bryan Wilson. There is a lot to be said for hurrying this book to the front-line of teaching as soon as possible.

A reinforcing example of the simplifications following on too sweeping a paradigm of secularization is available at this very moment and not merely in relation to the historical record. Wherever the world fails to travel safely to the prescribed secular destination, in places like Cairo or Dallas, it is held to suffer from retardation. Should vigorous movements of revitalization emerge all over the globe, they are often assembled inside a package of retardations and not infrequently labelled 'fundamentalist'. Thus, not only the 'new religious Right' in the United States but Jewish ultra-orthodoxy, communal tension in India, Pentecostalism all over the third world and Islamic revival can be brought together under the rubric of fundamentalism. A Western moral panic serves to organize perception of 'the other' and tends to do so in terms of reaction to secularization. Indeed, the largest single grant in the history of the discipline was dispensed precisely to understand the 'problem' of fundamentalism. By the same criteria, are not Catholicism and Islam 'problems' as such? Who is the problem? Who says who is the problem?

A final tendency associated with the problematic of secularization is really an extension of tendencies already mentioned. It is the emphasis on transitions, especially from tradition *to* modernity. It is not that the importance of modernity has been exaggerated, but that the treatment accorded to absolutely central historical movements, like the Reformation, the Counter-Reformation and the Renaissance, becomes stereotyped and skewed. When history seems to be consulted, it plays a bit part in the drama of modernization, and does not emerge in its own specific character. In particular, seen from the viewpoint of the student, the 'Protestant Ethic' is there to be tucked into rationalization and the advent of capitalism. Protestantism is linked to rationalization; the Society of Jesus, another candidate, is not. Both, however, present rich terrain for understanding religion in its time and place, not merely as a prelude to our own era. A rich and profound book setting all this in a quite different perspective is Gauchet's *The Disenchantment of the World* (1997).

In the case of Weber's (1930) 'Protestant Ethic' there have been plenty of critiques from within sociology as well as without, but it is still in constant reproduction, perhaps because it performs a particular theoretical job. Samuelsson (1961) provided one kind of critique, and such critiques have continued, almost *ad infinitum*, but what stays in the student's mind is a skewed version of Calvinism doing duty for all the reformations, even including the Radical Reformation.

One way to deal with this is to restore the specificity of history in and for its own sake. A major work which might revise the stereotypes and right the imbalances is Robert Wuthnow's (1989) *Communities of Discourse: Ideology and Social Structure in the Reformation, the Enlightenment and European Socialism.* Happily, this is by a sociologist, yet rests on a firm historical base. But what would also be valuable is some introduction to issues that simply illuminate the role of religion at a given time in a given place. Students need exposing to a whole range of different problematics, different analytic interests, different presuppositions, and modes of patterning material. They might even be offered unprotected exposure to history. For example, a reading of Geoffrey Elton's (1963) *Reformation Europe, 1517–1559* would expose students to a very trenchant treatment of precisely those theses about Protestantism which otherwise loom so large in their horizon. Or one might introduce them to the controversy over the English Reformation which has been fruitfully carried on since A. G. Dickens. If one wants to adduce a 'theoretical' justification for such a subject, then it does at least concern the early modern period of our own culture. The material is rich and instructive. It is about religion as such and shows how fragile some of our suppositions have been and are. A project examining such authors as Patrick Collinson, Eamonn Duffy, Christopher Haigh, Margaret Aston, Jack Scarisbrick, R. N.

Swanson and Richard Rex would open new worlds on the real workings of religion within a narrative texture, and illustrate the criteria and materials involved in coming to judgements. The historical debate over the Halévy (1937) thesis offers the same opportunities.

One further point is worth adding. In the humanities at the present time, scholarship makes full use of all possible disciplinary resources: art history, iconography, musicology, literature, liturgiology and so on. If we are not already doing this we should be.

The prime necessity of the historical

Sociologists of religion cannot be everywhere, doing everything. They are few in number, constrained in time and money. Their achievements are remarkable. So a critique such as this has to be tempered, especially since it includes a *mea culpa*. It amounts, so far, to the following. We have not paid enough attention to the religious mainstream, including the European mainstream. We have been limited as well as assisted by our major problematics, and have paid less attention than we should to meanings and ideas, and in particular bypassed historical particularity and variability as exemplified in time, place, context, narrative, events and persons. The particularities of the historical are constantly required to qualify the generalities of sociology. It is not that history is atheoretical, but that the theories of historians, apart from being more implicit, are fruitfully different from ours, and the practice of historians can assist us in achieving a fully cross-disciplinary approach. To reinforce that point an example is now offered of a historian dealing with a sociological topic.

The example offered is Linda Colley's (1992) *Britons: Forging the Nation 1707–1837*. Her topic is the construction of national identity and the argument turns on the pre-eminent role played by religion in turning peasants into patriots. Linda Colley shows how a popular Protestantism became the key element in British identity by dramatic contrast with Roman Catholic France. Particularly interesting is the use of iconography and art history in, for example, Hogarth's satirical aquatint of John Wilkes, S. M. W. Turner's *Slave Ship* and Wilkie's *Chelsea Pensioners reading the Gazette of the Battle of*

Waterloo 1822. But that is not to say that crucial shifts in demographics, or in the scale and dynamism of markets, or in military organization, are in any way played down. All the multitudinous interacting elements are held together in a narrative which shows what led to what. These elements include the role of central players like George III and also of millions of men and women whose individual motivations in the circumstances of their time, place and region made up the moving picture of nascent Britain. Region and social geography are plainly very important, and Colley draws precisely on the sociological concepts of centre and periphery to analyse (for example) the role of Scots in pushing out the frontiers of empire. What *is* absent, however, is any sense that religion is some kind of epiphenomenon masking a real social essence located elsewhere. There is no parachuting in of notions like the 'conscience collective' with all the extraneous philosophical baggage about religion being society and vice versa. Extraneous philosophy and pregnant tautology are eschewed, whereas concepts like centre and periphery are deployed because they yield further sense. Critical studies of Durkheim by, for example, Steven Lukes (1975) and William Pickering (1984) are particularly useful in this regard.

The underlying point is, if I may state a view, that when one comes to write an account in time and place and circumstance of multitudinous human strivings, certain sociological concepts, such as centre and periphery, are extraordinary fruitful, whereas philosophically based metanarratives or generalized prescriptions about the real and its disguises are not. They belong to an otiose overworld. Yet, as will be indicated again below, this world too often infiltrates our vocabulary, our root metaphors, our orchestration and selection of themes, our modes of stripping away masks.

Let me say it again. The object of this excursus on 'the historical' is to extend the range of the perspectives we deploy solely to render them adequate for our analytic objectives. In my view, that means opening up space for meaning, interpretation, narrative, locality, particularity, the initiative of persons and the creative guidance of different kinds of vision, including religious vision. In terms of fundamental approach, that need not mean decreasing the space available for other approaches since extension of the one is not contraction of the other. As much as anything, it means minding our language and asking certain critical questions concerning the explicit warrants for reductionism. A *critical* sociology is one which casts the eye of criticism in every direction.

Prime relevance of the political

Linda Colley's book not only serves to show how important it is to locate religion in its context of time and place, but also serves to introduce the next issue, which is the importance of relating the religious to the political. Whereas it is crucial to relate the sociology of religion to history from the point of view of approach, it is crucial to relate it to 'the political' from the point of view of substance.

The argument for this can be summarized briefly. Religion and politics share a common ground in the concept of power but appeal to different resources for its mobilization. Again, religion embodies a perspective which is more overtly principled and long-term, while politics embodies a perspective more overtly instrumental and focused on the immediate event and current situation. Again the prime focus of religion is on the language of personal priorities and the wholeness of the person, whereas the prime focus of politics concerns technically adumbrated measures to secure certain social conditions and something which has to be called the integrity of the state.

The difference can be put another way. The parable of Dives and Lazarus, the Rich Man and the Beggar, is part of a religious view which sets an aureole around the faces of the poor and around acts of charity, but it offers a very indirect guide to the specific conditions that give rise to different types of beggar, or to the opportunity costs involved in alternative policies for reducing beggary. Public prayers in churches do not normally discuss alternative policies.

Now, this brief attempt to distinguish between religion and politics is too simple precisely because there is a constant flow backwards and forwards across the two realms. Moreover, the regulation of that flow varies as between the major religions, for example Islam and Christianity, a point which might suggest how formative for whole civilizations the codes and languages of major religions are. The languages of religion and politics are closer in Islam than in Christianity.

The cross is counterposed to the sword, the power of love to the love of power. The good news concerns peace, goodwill and reconciliation. How is it, then, that the cross becomes the sword, both the sword of justice and the sword of national pride and imperial assertion? The cross stands on crusaders' shields and on national flags, as well as on hospitals and the vehicles of the International Red Cross. The cross as a sign of peace and of a non-violent individual sacrifice emerges in a thousand war cemeteries to commemorate mass sacrifice in war. Why?

There is another way to put this dialectic. Christianity rapidly came to constitute a universalization and spiritualization of fundamental social concepts: the land, the city, the kingdom, power and warfare. Jerusalem and Zion are 'above' and God's kingdom is expanded not by force but by the sword of the spirit. But for reasons which have to do with the nature of social integration and regulation, with the struggle for survival and for just relationships within and between social groups, this message has *in part* to mutate back again to its temporal location, in fresh earthly cities, in new 'holy lands', in godly nations or, for that matter, in the temporal politics of social gospel or liberation theology.

The above example is entirely sociological, since it has to do with the mutation of ideas in the furnace of social processes. It lies at a junction where religion and politics, faith and community are mutually and massively implicated together, and so illustrates the linkage of the religious and the political. But with only one shift of tonality, it could provide the structure of a theological argument.

That example suggests that some of the basic elements dealt with by sociology overlap some of the basic elements of theological discourse. They both deal with land, city, exodus, exile, transition, entry, warfare, power, sacrifice and so on, but whereas sociology traces webs of connection, theology reassembles these realities as a solid poetry concerned with imperatives of hope and necessary cost. These dramatic poles of hope and cost, vision and sacrifice, draw into their scope all the resources of emblem and image, for example, the sacrificial lamb and the visionary lion, crossings through waters of death and waters of life, journeys through wildernesses of testing to delectable mountains, the grass that withers and the rose that never fades. The primary emblems of light and darkness correspond almost exactly to hope and cost and to the underlying ground of everything – life and death, provided these are understood as complementary: the gift of life by a passage through death.

Perhaps this imagery begins to look as if it lies at some distance from sociology, but the common ground, in fact, remains even if treated in very different modes. Take, for example, the vocabulary of peace and violence, central to both. Sociology and theology both recognize a creative turbulence occurring as the power of the flood waters of religion effects a junction with the mainstreams of politics. Each discipline recognizes that peace and violence twist and turn in this maelstrom, the one turning into the other and vice versa. But sociology analyses the paradoxical interconnections while theology absorbs, dramatizes and images the paradoxes themselves as they are worked out in the stuff of human existence. Thus the enactments of faith are the social and human realities of peace and violence cast into a condensed drama in the intimate company of hope and cost, light and darkness, life and death, presence and absence. Taking only the strand of peace and violence, the eucharist is a re-presentation of the unity of peace and the violence of the broken body: the body of Christ, the body of his people, the body of the *polis* and of the peoples of the world. To put it another way, it is a union of love's helpless expense in pursuit of peace and of the spirit's recuperative power after violence. Peace and violence, love and power: is there a more fundamental vocabulary? It is here, of course, where an entry may be effected from sociology to theology, should one so desire (Martin, 1997).

Return to sociology proper?

The key sentence in the above was conditional: one could use this material to effect an entry into theology, *supposing* one wanted to effect it. But to do so lies outside the strictly limited contract established and agreed between teacher and student, which has to do with traceable social connections pursued in a secular context. The shift of tonality involved in effecting the entry into theology breaks that contract and deals with matters which are irrelevant to some students, even (maybe) offensive

David Martin

to others. If those matters are to be dealt with, there has to be a change of venue, a reassembly under a different and voluntary contract. But what could be reassembled under that different contract would not be marginal but fundamental.

Sociological analysis, existential concern

Still pursuing the 'creative turbulence' lying within the crucial relationships of the religious to the political, it would be useful to take an example illustrating the point about different contracts. This example looks at a particular set of religio-political problems to do with violence from a purely analytic viewpoint, but also indicates that among students themselves these problems give rise to moral and existential concern. Indeed, one has to recognize that their initial interest in such problems often derives, like one's own, from the challenge they present to frustrated utopianism or political commitment or religious understanding.

In my own teaching I place Northern Ireland, Bosnia, Lebanon, Israel, and the Caucasus in a common frame, because in each of these places religion is involved or appears to be involved, depending on what hermeneutic of suspicion is deployed, in internecine and inter-state violence on an appalling scale. The sociological issues could hardly be more central: relations between majorities and minorities and one minority and another, the logic of alliances ('my enemy's enemy is my friend'), colonialism (including the colonialism of ex-colonies), relations between rival imperial centres and their strategic peripheries and proxies, the institution of the feud pursued over many generations, the symbiosis of rival militias, male violence, the mobilization of repressed groups, the resuscitation and recitation of myths of communal hate, migrations, plantations, demographic rivalries, mystical and quasi-historical principles for defining borders, sacred memorials and locales for recollecting defeat and victory.

The language of confrontation, or at least of social identification, in situations such as those in Lebanon or Bosnia or Armenia often has a religious component: Christian, Shia, Sunni, Druze; Serb, Croat, Muslim; Jew, Muslim, Christian; Protestant and Catholic. And mixed up in the communal mayhem are world faiths whose central symbol is peace (*pax, salaam, shalom*) and whose central objective is the moral ordering of humankind. Clearly, the problem of mutation in the furnace of social processes is present once again. But, analytically, there is a further problem, which is that communal mayhem can occur to just the same degree in Rwanda or Somalia or Central Asia without any religious component whatever. All that such situations require is the existence of relations of majority–minority, superordination–subordination, identity–difference.

Once students are intellectually engaged by such a set of problems they sometimes give open expression to moral perplexity and even existential distress. Indeed, I recollect one student telling me she could not stand all that violence so could we not talk about India instead. Perplexity and concern of this kind can be recognized by a teacher. It does, after all, touch on fundamental understandings of the human condition, including the abyss of evil. But, presumably, actual discussion of the issue itself lies outside the limited and secular contract governing the classroom. Perhaps there should be some special institutional arrangement for responding to issues of this kind.

The imposition of frames and concepts

This essay has been clearly based on the argument that while there is, indeed, a shared core of rules about how we proceed in logical argument and adduce evidence to support hypotheses, we are engaged in a perspectival discipline. Certainly few of our propositions would perform well if subjected to the kind of 'covering law' procedure recommended by Carl Hempel (1970). Our worlds are commonsensical, contextual, saturated in the varied overtones of language and infiltrated by contrasting perspectives.

Unfortunately, most students are unaware of the varied presuppositions which underlie the discourses into which they are being inducted. They sense that the secure earth is shifting around them and that the straightforward commonsensicality of their world is being rendered precarious, but do not know precisely in what way. Given that these ways of rendering the world may themselves be fragile or philosophically debatable, it is only reasonable to help them appreciate this fragility. This may well be a difficult task, because students both need to know that there is an objective pressure deriving from evidence and argument and also that there is a certain fragility attaching to the master concepts, the root metaphors and the implied understandings of the human situation.

One way of dealing with the problem is to introduce them to the philosophy of science along a given range, say, from Feierabend to Hempel, and certainly including scholars such as Popper (1957), Lakatos and Musgrave (1970), Hesse (1980) and Michael Polanyi (1958). But this is far from easy. It may take up time more profitably used on other topics and could easily present difficulties to the philosophically disinclined. Perhaps little more can be achieved than some initial consciousness that we are dealing in likelihoods, not cut and dried propositions, and that the subject comes wrapped in philosophically rooted approaches to the world.

There are several areas where infiltration from philosophical presuppositions is particularly worth inspection. One is the way in which concepts like the 'conscience collective' are parachuted in from above to corral material on the ground. Thus, it is loosely implied that religion equals society and vice versa and a religious ceremony, for example, is re-viewed as a mysterious emanation of the collectivity. Another is the way explanations are taken out of sociological stock and applied to phenomena, particularly religious movements. Thus a religious movement will be seen both as remedying some lack and as offering a misguided solution to a problem located elsewhere. A prime example of this is the way religious movements are automatically seen as politics in fantastic disguise, preventing 'real' action, leading to a cul-de-sac, and above all waiting for release in the natural channel of politics.

The phrase 'the natural channel of politics' introduces yet another way in which presuppositions are introduced: the deployment of root metaphors. Unfortunately, lying behind most sociological discourse are a few root metaphors, some organic, some mechanistic. These metaphors are more than decorative or colourful aids to rapid apprehension, though admittedly some are used merely to upgrade discourse and impart a scientistic gloss. The point is that students would gain from having some sense of the queries that can be placed against organicist or mechanistic root metaphors. In the words of Morris Ginsberg (personal conversation): 'Societies don't function, they just stagger along.' Many of these metaphors serve to ease the path of questionable translations of religion into the language of 'the social'.

At the same time, in the ordinary course of sociological analysis, one does not need to draw on the world of root metaphors. Thus, in the example offered earlier of the elements involved in religio-political situations in Bosnia or the Lebanon, there is no need to induce too chronic a sense of high-level infiltration from the presuppositions of theory. The relations of majority and minority, subordination and superordination are observables operating at the middle-range level and not particularly problematic. If not totally safe they are reasonably convincing.

A wider literature

Beyond the standard curricula accessible to students there are other literatures which bear on the sociology of religion and alter the horizon within which it is understood. There is, first of all, a literature mostly situated in the political domain which bears insightfully on the space of religion. Amongst major contributions to this literature are the critical theorists, eccentric Marxists like Gramsci, and a figure like Georges Sorel whose *Reflections on Violence* constitutes a classic in the sociology of religion (Sorel, 1961).

Then there is a literature which bears on questions of philosophical anthropology undeniably adjacent to the sociology of religion by scholars such as Eric Voegelin and Hans Jonas. Useful introductions to them and others are to be found in *Realism: An Essay in Interpretation and Social Reality* (Levy, 1981) and *The Measure of Man* (Levy, 1993). A final category consists of books which bear critically on the sociology of religion from a philosophical viewpoint. One which happens to be suitable for students and deals *inter alia* with religious theories of religion is *Religion Defined and Explained* (Byrne and Clarke, 1993). Another which is not suitable for undergraduates is *Theology and Social Theory* (Milbank, 1990), a wide-ranging critique of the very existence of a sociology of religion.

Concluding pastoral reflection

This pastoral reflection has to do with the language we use from the podium and the teaching authority we deploy, in the context of a multi-cultural society. A given class might well include a black Pentecostal woman, a devout Jew or Muslim, an Adventist, a recently converted evangelical, an Irish Catholic, a New Age practitioner. This means that teachers address people with very different commitments and sensitivities, and common courtesy suggests these need to be taken into account.

Clearly, there is an intellectual authority inherent in expertise and experience and equally clearly it is impossible to temper the requirements of logical or empirical inference to the varying cultural sensibilities of students. Everybody is controlled by the same rules of argument. At the same time, our language carries all kinds of implications which do not so much reflect that shared ground of logic and evidence as derive from particular perspectives. Thus, for example, there are evolutionary or developmental perspectives clearly implying that this or that religious form is behind, or somehow retarded within a premodern phase, or reactionary. Though the Whig version of history may be thoroughly disavowed by historians it remains a pervasive presence in our language and preconceptions, and students may well react with shock and distress.

When teachers become aware that some students are shocked by the abrasions of the language we use to analyse religion, or are disturbed by alien root metaphors or evolutionary schemes, they might consider making available texts which adopt a more sympathetic tone or evoke sympathetically the particular world from which the student comes. Examples might help. If a young Irishman shows signs of being pressured, or even if he does not, by a residual Whiggery in our accounts of social evolution, then it is perfectly reasonable to put him in the way of historiography after Butterfield. Again, if a black Pentecostal woman shows signs of discomfort at reductive accounts of religion in terms of compensators, one might suggest Sidney Mintz's (1974) *Worker in the Cane* or Elaine Lawless' recent studies of Pentecostal women preachers in rural America (for example, Lawless, 1988).

There exists a double duty: on the one hand gently to expand sealed social worlds, on the other quietly to indicate what intellectually respectable defences students might care to use. These are the courtesies which both educate in the sense of 'drawing out', and which also respect the intellectual rights of others.

References

Badham, P. (ed.) (1987), *Religion, State and Society in Modern Britain*, Lampeter, Edwin Mellen Press.

Bailey, E. I. (1997), *Implicit Religion in Contemporary Society*, Kampen, Netherlands, Kok Pharos.

Beckford, J. (1989), *Religion and Advanced Industrial Society*, London, Unwin Hyman.

Berger, P. (1969), *The Social Reality of Religion*, London, Faber & Faber.

Berger, P. and Luckmann, T. (1966), *The Social Construction of Reality*, Garden City, New York, Doubleday.

Bowker, J. (1995), *Is God a Virus?* London, SPCK.

Braudel, F. (1991), *The Identity of France*, London, Fontana.

Bruce, S. (ed.) (1992), *Religion and Modernization*, Oxford, Clarendon Press.

Burke, K. (1984), *Permanence and Change: An Anatomy of Purpose*, Berkeley, University of California Press.

Butler, J. (1990), *Awash in a Sea of Faith*, Cambridge, Massachusetts, Harvard University Press.

Butterfield, H. (1957), *Christianity and History*, London, Fontana.

Byrne, P. and Clarke, P. (1993), *Religion Defined and Explained*, Basingstoke, Macmillan.

Casanova, J. (1994), *Public Religions in the Modern World*, Chicago, University of Chicago Press.

Casserley, J. V. L. (1951), *Morals and Man in the Social Sciences*, London and New York, Longmans, Green.

Chadwick, O. (1975), *The Secularization of the European Mind in the Nineteenth Century*, Cambridge, Cambridge University Press.

Colley, L. (1992), *Britons: Forging the Nation 1707–1837*, New Haven, Yale University Press.

Connerton, P. (1989), *How Societies Remember*, Cambridge, Cambridge University Press.

Davie, G. (1994), *Religion in Britain since 1945*, Oxford, Blackwell.

Davies, J. and Wollaston, I. (eds) (1993), *A Sociology of Sacred Texts*, Sheffield, Sheffield Academic Press.

David Martin

Dawkins, R. (1995), *River out of Eden*, London, Weidenfeld & Nicholson.

Eisenstadt, S. N. (1956), *From Generation to Generation: Age Groups and Social Structure*, London, Routledge & Kegan Paul.

Eisenstadt, S. N. (1973), *Tradition, Change and Modernity*, New York, Wiley-Interscience.

Ellul, J. (1964), *The Technological Society*, New York, Knopf.

Elton, G. (1963), *Reformation Europe, 1517–1559*, London, Fontana.

Emmet, D. and MacIntyre, A. (1970), *Sociological Theory and Philosophical Analysis*, London, Macmillan.

Fenn, R. K. (1992), *The Death of Herod*, Cambridge, Cambridge University Press.

Fingarette, H. (1963), *The Self in Transformation: Psychoanalysis, Philosophy and the Life of the Spirit*, New York, Basic Books.

Firth, R. (1973), *Symbols: Public and Private*, London, Allen & Unwin.

Fortes, M. and Bourdillon, M. F. C. (eds) (1980), *Sacrifice*, London, Academic Press.

Friedman, M. and Heilman, S. C. (1994), Religious fundamentalism and religious Jews, in M. Marty and R. S. Appleby (eds), *Fundamentalism Observed*, pp. 197–264, Chicago, University of Chicago Press.

Gauchet, M. (1997), *The Disenchantment of the World*, Princeton, Princeton University Press.

Gellner, E. (1992), *Postmodernism, Reason and Religion*, London, Routledge.

Gifford, P. (1998), *African Christianity: The Public Role*, London, Hurst.

Halbwachs, M. (1950), *La Mémoire Collective*, Paris, Presses Universitaires de France.

Halbwachs, M. (1976), *Les Cadres Sociaux de la Mémoire*, Paris, La Haye, Mouton.

Halévy, E. (1937), *A History of the English People in 1815*, London, Penguin.

Hauerwas, S. (1988), *Suffering Presence*, Edinburgh, T. & T. Clark.

Heelas, P., Lash, S. and Morris, P. (eds) (1995), *Detraditionalisation: Authority and Identity in an Age of Cultural Uncertainty*, Oxford, Blackwell.

Hempel, C. G. (1970), *Aspects of Scientific Explanation and Other Essays in the Philosophy of Science*, New York, Free Press.

Hervieu-Léger, D. (1986), *Vers un Nouveau Christianisme: Introduction à la Sociologie du Christianisme Occidental*, Paris, Cerf.

Hervieu-Léger, D. (1993), *La Religion pour Mémoire*, Paris, Cerf.

Hesse, M. (1980), *Revolutions and Reconstructions in the Philosophy of Science*, Notre Dame, Notre Dame University Press.

Hodges, H. A. (1944), *Wilhelm Dilthy: An Introduction*, London, Routledge.

Hulme, T. E. (1960), *Speculations*, London, Routledge.

Hynes, S. (1968), *The Edwardian Turn of Mind*, Princeton, Princeton University Press.

Lakatos, I. and Musgrave, A. (eds) (1970), *Criticism and the Growth of Knowledge*, Cambridge, Cambridge University Press.

Lawless, E. (1988), *Handmaidens of the Lord: Pentecostal Women Preachers and Traditional Religion*, Philadelphia, University of Philadelphia Press.

Lerner, D. (1958), *The Passing of Traditional Society*, Chicago, Free Press.

Levine, D. (1992), *Popular Voices in Latin American Catholicism*, Princeton, Princeton University Press.

Levy, D. (1981), *Realism: An Essay in Interpretation and Social Reality*, Manchester, Carcanet.

Levy, D. (1993), *The Measure of Man*, Columbia, University of Missouri Press.

Lewis, I. M. (1976), *Social Anthropology in Perspective: The Relevance of Social Anthropology*, Harmondsworth, Penguin.

Luckmann, T. (1967), *The Invisible Religion*, New York, Macmillan.

Lukes, S. (1975), *Emile Durkheim*, Harmondsworth, Peregrine Books.

MacIntyre, A. (1981), *After Virtue: A Study in Moral Theory*, London, Duckworth.

MacIntyre, A. (1988), *Whose Justice? Which Rationality?* London, Duckworth.

Mannheim, K. (1952), Conservative thought, in *Essays on the Sociology of Knowledge*, pp. 74–164, London, Routledge.

Mannheim, K. (1982), The problem of generations, in *Essays on the Sociology of Knowledge*, pp. 276–320, London, Routledge.

Markham, I. (1994), *Plurality and Christian Ethics*, Cambridge, Cambridge University Press.

Marsden, G. (1990), *Religion and American Culture*, New York, Harcourt Brace Jovanovich.

Marsden, G. (1994), *The Soul of the American University*, Oxford, Oxford University Press.

Marsden, G. and Longfield, B. (1993), *The Secularization of the Academy*, Oxford, Oxford University Press.

Martin, B. (1981), *A Sociology of Contemporary Cultural Change*, Oxford, Blackwell.

Martin, D. (1978), *A General Theory of Secularization*, Oxford, Blackwell.

Martin, D. (1990), *Tongues of Fire*, Oxford, Blackwell.

David Martin

Martin, D. (1997), *Reflections on Sociology and Theology*, Oxford, Clarendon Press.

Mead, G. H. (1934), *Mind, Self and Society*, Chicago, University of Chicago Press.

Milbank, J. (1990), *Theology and Social Theory*, Oxford, Blackwell.

Mills, C. W. (1959), *The Sociological Imagination*, Oxford, Oxford University Press.

Mintz, S. (1974), *Worker in the Cane*, New York, Norton.

Mitchell, B. (1980), *Morality: Religious and Secular*, Oxford, Clarendon Press.

Mitchell, B. (1994), *Faith and Criticism*, Oxford, Clarendon Press.

Moyser, G. and Medhurst, K. (1988), *Church and Politics in a Secular Age*, Oxford, Clarendon Press.

Pickering, W. (1984), *Durkheim's Sociology of Religion: Themes and Theories*, London, Routledge.

Polanyi, M. (1958), *Personal Knowledge*, London, Routledge.

Popper, K. (1957), *The Poverty of Historicism*, London, Routledge.

Ricoeur, P. (1976), *Integration Theory: Discourse and the Surplus of Meaning*, Fort Worth, Texas Christian University Press.

Robertson, R. (1978), *Meaning and Change: Explorations in the Cultural Sociology of Modern Societies*, Oxford, Blackwell.

Robertson, R. (1992), *Globalization: Social Theory and Global Culture*, London, Sage Publications.

Rose, J. (1986), *The Edwardian Temperament 1895–1919*, Cleveland, Ohio University Press.

Sallnow, M. and Eade, J. (1991), *Contesting the Sacred: The Anthropology of Christian Pilgrimage*, London, Routledge.

Samuelsson, K. (1961), *Religion and Economic Action*, New York, Heinemann Basic Books.

Shils, E. (1981), *Tradition*, London, Faber & Faber.

Skinner, B. F. (1972), *Beyond Freedom and Dignity*, London, Jonathan Cape.

Sorel, G. (1961), *Reflections on Violence*, New York, Collier Books.

Stark, R. and Bainbridge, W. S. (1987), *The Theory of Religion*, New York, Lang.

Stark, R. and Bainbridge, W. S. (1985), *The Future of Religion*, Berkeley, University of California Press.

Stark, R. and Finke, R. (1986), Turning pews into people: estimating nineteenth-century church membership, *Journal for the Scientific Study of Religion*, 25, 180–92.

Starkey, D. (1978), *Parallel or Divergence: Monarchical Symbolism in England During the Reformation and After*, Acts of the 14th conference of the CISR (Strasbourg 1977), CISR, Lille.

Thomas, T. (ed.) (1988), *The British: Their Religious Beliefs and Practices 1800–1986*, London, Routledge.
Thompson, E. P. (1968), *The Making of the English Working Class*, London, Gollancz.
Tiryakian, E. (1962), *Sociology and Existentialism*, Englewood Cliffs, New Jersey, Prentice Hall.
Turner, B. (1983), *Religion and Social Theory*, London, Heinemann Educational.
Turner, B. and Hepworth, M. (1982), *Confession*, London, Routledge.
Turner, V. (1974), *Dramas, Fields and Metaphors: Symbolic Action in Human Society*, Ithaca, Cornell University Press.
von Hayek, F. A. (1967), *Studies in Philosophy, Politics and Economics*, London, Routledge.
Walter, T. (ed.) (1999), *Mourning for Diana*, Oxford, Berg.
Webb, R. K. (1980), *Modern England from the Eighteenth Century to the Present*, London, Allen and Unwin.
Weber, M. (1930), *The Protestant Ethic and the Spirit of Capitalism*, London, Unwin University Books.
Wertheimer, J. (1992), *The Uses of Tradition: Jewish Continuity in the Modern Era*, New York, Jewish Theological Seminary of America.
Wuthnow, R. (1989), *Communities of Discourse: Ideology and Social Structure in the Reformation, the Enlightenment and European Socialism*, Cambridge, Massachusetts, Harvard University Press.
Wuthnow, R. (1993), *Christianity in the Twenty-first Century*, Oxford, Oxford University Press.

2

A Theological Response to Sociology

Ronald Preston

Introduction

I am in general agreement with David Martin's paper, so that though this is a response to it, in a sense it could stand on its own. He writes primarily as a sociologist, I write primarily as a theologian. Approaching from this different stance, my primary purpose is to support his main contentions.

Martin is both a professional sociologist and also no mean 'lay' theologian; I am a professional theologian, but not a sociologist. However, I was trained in economics, which is also a social science, and I have had an interest ever since in the relation of theology to the social sciences. I have, of course, read a good deal of sociology, but that is not the same thing as being trained in it; and I make no pretence of possessing sociological expertise. I conceive that my task is to make a theological response to sociology, parallel to a primarily sociological approach to theology made by Martin.

Sociology and theology

Even if a sociologist can come to conservative conclusions, sociology is an inherently radical discipline. It is radical because it brings analytical techniques to bear on social structures and institutions which many people take for granted, especially if they are broadly 'establishment' folk. Institutions which are generally considered the foundation of society are critically examined; the law, the church, the nation state, the monarchy. Many are startled when the church in particular comes under this scrutiny, because an aura of holiness tends to surround all its structures, suggesting that it is impious to subject them to critical examination. The Curia in the Roman Catholic Church is an example.

There is nothing mysterious in the methods of sociology. Martin says all that is mandatory is logical inference, coherence, and criteria for assessing evidence. This last requirement does in fact raise some difficulties, as the criteria brought to bear on an enquiry affect what is considered relevant evidence and the weight to be given to different elements in it; but Martin and I agree that the criteria can in principle be accepted by all those writing in a 'liberal' university, about which I shall write below.

On the basis mentioned by Martin, sociologists raise questions in a systematic way over the whole range of human interactions, largely unthought of before the subject was developed. They are particularly alert to the unintended secondary consequences of human collective activities. What of the influence of individuals? Sociologists have no socio-logical grounds for excluding the influence of particular persons on social processes, as Martin stresses, any more than they have for using a quasi-determinist vocabulary in their work. These are assumptions brought into sociology by some sociologists, they do not arise out of it. Sociologists have to be as careful as economists in scrutinizing the presuppositions on which they work. Hence a sociology of sociologists develops as a changing social milieu has subtle effects on attitudes. Fashions have in fact powerfully influenced sociology. According to Flanagan (1996, p. 188):

> Reflection on the sociological condition points to a catalogue of most curious transmogrifications in its disciplinary history from the sociologist as superhero of positivist science, into chronicler of progress, into *angst* ridden advocate of the underclass, into concerned agent for social improvement, into prophet of the counterculture reading the spirit of the times, then flitting off into engaged but confused

commentary on the mass explosion of cultural studies, then turning into *flâneur* to see cosmopolitan culture, then ending up as a pilgrim.

It is no wonder that theology has questions to put to sociology.

Theology, however, has its own problems. It is a group of disciplines, linguistic, literary, historical, philosophical, psychological, and sociological. Indeed, the only intellectual activity it does not employ is experimental laboratory work. It is therefore impossible to isolate it from other disciplines. It, like them, is influenced by changing culture and intellectual trends, and properly so. Theology must be sensitive to its social milieu, not least because it often throws up new and important questions about human existence which need to be attended to if theology is not to become fossilized. At present it is issues which postmodernism throws up which dominate the scene. But both theology and sociology need to keep their heads, remembering the aphorism of Dean Inge, 'He who marries the spirit of the age soon finds himself a widower.' Christian theology has resources in the biblical witness to the transcendence of God, though the rigidity of church institutions has often had the effect of making it culture bound.

What is the core of Christian theology? Religion is such a protean phenomenon that I do not want to get diverted into a huge comparative analysis. I confine myself to the main religions of the world, and within them to Christianity, which is the main context of the present discussion, even in our present-day pluralist society. The main faiths appeal to a revelatory core, and these differ. Even Christianity itself is a protean phenomenon, and there are differences within it about the nature and extent of the core revelatory claims. In Christianity a priority is given to the Bible and to what Christians have made of it down the centuries, what is called 'tradition'. The tools of theology are in principle no different from those of any other discipline in the humanities, including sociology. But it is a tricky subject in universities and colleges of higher education because it deals with the whole range of human life at a deep personal and social level, including in its range the possibility of eternal life; and also because of the rival interpretations within it. Moreover, it now operates in a pluralist society in which other religions are significantly represented. And the fact that some university colleges are church related does not remove them from the difficulties raised by theology, and the colleges themselves are subject to sociological investigations. This is the background against which a discussion of sociology and theology has to take place. I intend in this response to look into the background and present position of Christian theology in higher education, with particular reference to the sociology of religion.

Historical perspective

In Europe we have inherited a Christendom situation, the only civilization in which the Christian tradition has built itself into the social structures. In the universities divinity professors were given a precedence over all others. A few remnants of this still survive in the UK. However, the whole Christendom situation has almost broken down and what remnants remain, as in the Irish Republic, are feeble compared with what they were, and are getting feebler. In its heyday the Church had great influence in the intellectual realm, but its record was not a good one. The treatment of Galileo can serve as an example of what went wrong. After the wars of religion, it was the Enlightenment that taught the virtue of tolerance and freedom of enquiry, and that tolerance did not mean indifference to truth but a commitment to explore it. Against this background there was a fear of theology and of the dangers of church control when the universities in this country expanded in the nineteenth century. Moreover, Christians were notoriously hostile to one another, and they combined in being hostile to Jews.

At Liverpool University, theology was ruled out by charter, until a fairly recent revision, because of the fear of conflict between Protestant and Roman Catholic. The nearest Liverpool University got to theology was Hellenistic Greek. At Manchester, in discussions prior to the founding of the faculty of theology in 1904 it was fear of Anglican and Free Church quarrels which caused hesitation. The senate would only consider proposals to which the various denominational theological seminaries in Manchester had assented. Further, comparative religion was made a compulsory subject because it was felt that otherwise Christians could not be trusted to take other religions seriously. Other features betray the nervousness at the time and the problems of handling it. Christian ethics got into the syllabus from the start because it was thought to be an uncontroversial and undogmatic subject. The university refused to teach doctrine but came to a compromise whereby it agreed to examine the history of doctrine. For a long time there was a statement in black type in the prospectus of the faculty to the effect that nothing would be taught which was reasonably offensive to the conscience of any student. What happens when, for instance, a Jewish student arrives who refuses to admit any error at all in the Massoretic text of the Hebrew Bible?

As time went on it became clear that the fears had been greatly exaggerated, and that there was no more difficulty in theology departments between rival schools of thought than there is in other disciplines, philosophy for one. However, the study of theology in the universities developed slowly. Between the wars biblical studies made an entry in one or two places, but it was only after 1945 that substantial growth occurred in the number of universities where theology and religious studies is available, covering a wide range of options. This comparatively successful accomplishment is now under attack, as we shall shortly see.

There is no suggestion in any of this that theology could be considered the queen of the sciences. The churches could not maintain their traditional intellectual position and power of control. Not only the natural sciences had to break away, but so also did political theory and economics.[1] As an example, in economics a treatment of usury had been crippled by a combination of biblical texts and the virtual canonization of Aristotle. It was not until the eighteenth century that a reconstruction of the foundations took place (though in practice the old theory had long been ignored). The new science of economics had to work out its own framework from scratch.

Three attacks

Sociology began in the nineteenth century as a discipline consciously needing to evade ecclesiastical control, though it has not been as successful in liberating itself from various 'faith' presuppositions as has the pure theory of economics. The earlier quotation from Flanagan is evidence of that.

Nevertheless, sociology has fitted in pretty well within the broad assumptions of the 'liberal' university, which I am about to consider. But before that I propose to mention three attacks on both which have come from the side of Christian theology in this century. (I confine myself to Britain.)

The first came from the Christendom group in the Church of England. It was an attempt to restore theology to the status of queen of the sciences by establishing a Christian sociology and in the light of it a Christian economics. It had a considerable reputation in Anglican circles, especially in 'high church' circles. Founded in 1924 it flourished in the 1930s, but had exhausted itself by about 1950. Its contention was that sociology as a discipline in British universities operated on assumptions, avowed or implicit, which are incompatible with Christian faith, particularly in its doctrine of man (*sic*). An alternative Christian sociology had to be created.

A year after I graduated I went to a discussion between V. A. Demant, the leading Christendom thinker, and Morris Ginsberg, the doyen of British sociologists, who held the Martin White Chair in Sociology at the London School of Economics. They talked past one another. It was a dialogue of the deaf. David Martin is quite right in saying that there is no possibility of reviving the Christendom stance. But that does not mean Ginsberg has the last word, as more recent theological challenges to the 'liberal' university show.

A second and formidable challenge has come recently from John Milbank's *Theology and Social Theory* (1990). In the context of the postmodern intellectual mood of the last two decades he takes the view that the different 'faith' presuppositions of today are incompatible, so that neither theology nor any other faith or philosophy can be queen of the sciences. The important point is that theology should be queen of Christian social theory. It is a major book in the genre of the history of ideas. I summarize its basic arguments.

Milbank attacks any alliance between theology and any humanistic social theory. Religion is so fundamental that we cannot get behind it into any more general category in which it can be fitted. Those who try to relate theology to sociology in this way are turning sociology into a theology and a church in disguise. Postmodernism and deconstruction have undermined any general social theory. We are in a world of incompatible truth claims. Theology must realize this. We must make a choice and declare our allegiance to one particular tradition (he, of course, is concerned with the Christian one), and then study reality in the light of it. Secular theories cannot be refuted. They can only be out-narrated by the Christian story. There is no neutral, rational account of society available. There can be no neutral sociology. Theology can be queen again of its own domain, as it bears the marks of reason illuminated by the incarnation and Pentecost, and it can expose all other cultural and social theories as threatened by nihilism, *provided* that Christianity is itself self-critical.

Is it indeed the case that different faith traditions have nothing in common and exclude in their several theories what is held by others? (Note that secularism and secular humanism are faiths in the sense in which the term is being used.) In my judgement the answer must be No. Martin agrees. One of the main points of his presentation is that the Christian under-standing of the human profoundly overlaps with humanist and existentialist ones. But Martin adds his own warning to sociology when he refers to any reductionism which would subsume human beings entirely within their social relations.

The Christian drama from Genesis to Revelation is a powerful interpretation of human nature and human destiny, part myth and part history. So is its picture of Christian living in a sacramental community between the now of Christ's victory over sin and death and the *not yet* of his final triumph. But when we consider its implications for how Christians should behave to one another, and as Christians to those of other faiths and philosophies, not only in their personal dealings, but also the social structures they should work for, it becomes clear that a theology of civil society is needed. The Bible presupposes a civil society without being prescriptive about its details. It is not a text book of political theory.

Universities are structures within civil society. Christians should expect to find much common ground on the basis of which they have a call to work with others in the cause of human flourishing, which is God's will for all men and women, not just Christians. What I shall shortly discuss about the 'liberal' university is based on this affirmation. I think Milbank's position is very dangerous as the basis of a Christian social theology.

A third theological attack, in this case on the present position of theology in the universities, has come from an article by Gavin D'Costa (1996), 'The end of "theology" and "religious studies"'. He also is much influenced by postmo-dern-ist intellectual tendencies. He contends that theology of its nature is alien to the secular universities. If it appears in the guise of religious studies a dubious neutrality between religions is assumed. Christian theology needs to be carried on in a Christian setting, as a university setting imposes alien criteria. In that setting students cannot be taught to use their theology to think theologically.[2] 'Liberal' university teachers will think they must bracket out their own convictions. Postmodernist ones will also react against this, maintaining that objectivity and neutrality are impossible. Indeed, there is no universal rationality. The Christian narrative must interpret the world, not let the world interpret it. His conclusion is that religious studies should be set within the framework of systematic theology. So there will be a series of different theological and religious studies according to the different presuppositions of the various faiths. Each will make clear its own presupposi-tions. Then theology and religious studies in the university will be a federation of parallel disciplines. If this is dismissed as sectarian, the reply is that it is good sectarianism.

The obvious practical difficulty of this is that no British university would finance such fragmentation. More important, such a proposal would be as intellectually and existentially disastrous in the present scene as Milbank's proposal to which it has a clear affinity. It is a denial that there is a common human experience on which religion can comment and endeavour to illuminate.

The university

To grasp this let us ask what a university must be committed to if it is to be true to itself. This is an important question because it is rarely asked in the continuing debate on higher education in the public forum, or in the university itself. Sixty years ago it came to the fore acutely with the collapse of the German universities when faced with the challenge of Nazism (the churches on the whole did not do much better, but their muddied record is another story). What should the German universities have stood for? What should they in the last resort have been prepared to suffer, and even die, for? This is a relevant question for all university folk, Christians, and adherents of various humanist faiths as well as those of other religions. It involves a combination of intellectual values, and moral values which are closely connected with them.

It must involve honesty in the intellectual quest, not cooking the evidence, careful attention to opposing positions, and dialoguing with them, stating them as accurately as possible without caricaturing them, being as self-conscious as possible about one's own presuppositions, and not prescribing conclusions in advance. These are some of the essentials of free enquiry. I think that Christians must stand for them in tertiary education.

How does theology fit into this? It must surely support these essentials of free enquiry. If it does, it is entitled to be considered a serious subject of study, and not to be superciliously dismissed, as sometimes by secularists, as the study of an alleged reality, now outdated, like the phlogiston theory in chemistry in the eighteenth century. It must be considered a subject worth pursuing, and that will include a study of the community out of which it springs.

Must a theological don believe in God? I once thought so, but now I do not. There are several examples known to me of very perceptive teachers of theology who are not believers, and one or two who have ceased being believers but are still perceptive theologians. It is the commitment to serious enquiry which is the key necessity.

It follows that the Christian responsibility for higher education in our contemporary society should not be to use the university for church or denominational intellectual power struggles, but to care for the inherent quality of what is being taught and researched, and the community in which these activities are carried on. Christians should help the university to fulfil its true vocation within God's intention for a humane civil society. It is not to promote a 'Christian' university, if it means one in which Christianity is in a position of privilege. For one thing it would prevent Christians from obtaining enlightenment from other faiths and philosophies at their best, not with the odds stacked against them. Christians should want a community in higher education in which, as students of any discipline, they will find the deepest intellectual and moral issues of life explored, directly or indirectly, in which presuppositions are made plain and explored in an atmosphere of seriousness and freedom.

The same criteria should apply with the same force in colleges of higher education directly related to the churches. They ought to be a beacon, but their history indicates that they have not always been, and are not always so today. There has been too much intellectual timidity and contentment with less than first-class standards. When they do collaborate with others in the tasks of higher education, the best contribution that Christian institutions can make is to provide opportunities for Christian worship. Indeed it is a distinctive contribution; no one else can make it. But it needs to be worship which, while focused on the central mysteries of the Christian faith, is specifically related to the particular concerns of academic life and its various disciplines. It is all too rare for the worship of Christian undergraduates and dons to be in this perspective, whether they worship separately or together.

Sociology of religion

And now I come to the sociology of religion as a discipline of particular interest when discussing theology and sociology. What does theology ask of it? In my judgement no more than a methodological agnosticism on the truth claims of religious belief, as distinct from whatever may be the personal beliefs of the sociologist. This means, however, that it must be clearly acknowledged that there is nothing in sociological theory or methods which entitle it to assume that religion is exhausted without remainder when sociologists have studied it as far as their discipline can take them. There is nothing in sociological method as such which entitles it to assume that religion is on the way out, as Marx assumed, or as much sociology has in fact assumed. It has given a particular interpretation of the steady development of industrialization, technological development, and urbanization which has been too dependent on doubtful assumptions in interpreting the data. The contrasting interpretations of broadly agreed data by Davie (1994) and Bruce (1995) are cases in point.

Sociologists of religion should pay more attention to the

Ronald Preston

'church' type of religious activity, to refer to Troeltsch's (1931) famous distinction between the 'church' type and the 'sect' type, a typology which has been considerably refined, but is still useful. Sociology of religion has fruitfully studied sects, but has been unduly preoccupied with them, partly because they are easier to encompass and study than the 'large institution', the study of which David Martin urges in his paper. The great church is, of course, a large institution. It has to combine two tasks which would seem a sociological impossibility within Troeltsch's typology. It has to have a thoroughly committed core at the heart of its congregations, and at the same time it has to take on anyone who turns up, regardless of their level of understanding or lack of it, and of their depth of commitment. It will have a large 'fringe' if it is doing its job. Of course it will be far from completely succeeding in this task. Much more study is needed of the 'great churches' in relation to this task, taking account of what they must stand for, but which will demand more than they will ever succeed in accomplishing. Church leaders and congregations need the help of sociology in general and the sociology of religion in particular to throw a light on their task which theology by itself cannot throw. For one thing it would save them from much frustration.[3]

References

Bruce, S. (1995), *Religion in Modern Britain*, Oxford, Oxford University Press.

Davie, G. (1994), *Religion in Britain since 1945: Believing without Belonging*, Oxford, Blackwell.

D'Costa, G. (1996), The end of 'theology' and 'religious studies', *Theology*, 99, 338–51.

Fairchild, H. N. (ed.) (1952), *Religious Perspectives in College Teaching*, New York, Ronald Press Co.

Flanagan, K. (1996), *The Enchantment of Sociology: A Study of Theology and Culture*, London, Macmillan.

Milbank, J. (1990), *Theology and Social Theory*, Oxford, Blackwell.

Moberly, W. (1949), *The Crisis in the University*, London, SCM Press.

Nash, A. (1944), *The University in the Modern World*, London, SCM Press.

Troeltsch, E. (1931), *The Social Teachings of the Christian Churches*, London, Allen & Unwin.

Notes

1. The recent social encyclicals of the Papacy do not squarely face the problem. They show a welcome tendency to stress the need of enlisting the help of the social sciences, but tacitly assume that what they produce will agree with the teaching of the magisterium.
2. Flanagan (1996) takes a similar position. Roman Catholics should not study theology at the university. It is a neutered discipline. Sociology is safer.
3. Towards the end of the 1939–45 war there was a major predecessor of the Engaging the Curriculum project in several countries, particularly the UK and the USA. The key books were those of Fairchild, Moberly and Nash mentioned in the references. The article in the Fairchild book on 'Sociology and social psychology' was written by Talcott Parsons. There are two chapters particularly relevant to the present project in *Christian Thinking and Social Order: Conviction Politics from the 1930s to the Present Day*, edited by Marjorie Reeves (Cassell, 1999). One is by me and one by Dr Harry Judge, but the whole book has relevance.

Part II   Theoretical Perspectives

3

Theological Reflection and Sociological Method

Andrew Dawson

Introduction

T hat 'all theology is situated' (Libânio, 1991, p. 49) is a
dictum familiar to those who have examined the interface
of theological reflection and sociological method. Indeed,
writing at a time when the treasures of sociology had yet to
be fully plundered by the theological community, Tillich (1951,
pp. 63–4) readily acknowledged that:

> It is always possible to show that all the rites,
> doctrines, institutions, and symbols of a religious
> system constitute a religious culture which is derived
> from the surrounding general culture – from its
> social and economic structure, its character traits, its
> opinions and philosophy, its linguistic and artistic
> expressions, its complexes, its traumas, and its
> longings.

The recognition of the derivative nature of theological language
inevitably leads theologians to concern themselves with the
manner and extent to which the theological endeavour is in
epistemological continuity with the given milieu in which such
theoretical labour takes place. As will be shown below, it is this
epistemological continuity which theology has with its given
milieu that generates a need for sociological insight, while also

furnishing the means by which sociological methods, assumptions, values, and conclusions may be critiqued. In short, this chapter seeks to demonstrate that there exists an umbilical tie between theological reflection and sociological method; a tie to the mutual benefit of each.

Double location

The manner in which the social and intellectual environment sets the epistemological parameters to theological articulation is approached by Bonino (1983, pp. 42–4) via the concept of 'double location'. If we are to comprehend the theological perspective of any thinker, maintains Bonino, we must first *situate* that thinker within two fundamentally interpenetrative, but analytically discrete *loci*. On the one hand, the theologian stands within a particular theoretical discipline, with its own peculiar epistemological conditions and methodological demands. We might say that any theologian stands within a very broad disciplinary paradigm constituted by a collectivity of 'first principles' particular to itself in terms of content and order (Kuhn, 1962, pp. 43–51). Such is the 'theological location'. On the other hand, the theologian remains at all times a social actor within a given historico-cultural and economico-political context. While never fully determinative of the nature and content of human self-conscious reflectivity, the 'social location' nevertheless furnishes both the empirical conditions of possibility within which thought occurs and the relevant material upon which theology reflects. In Mannheim's (1952) terms, all knowledge is relational; that is, knowledge is from a certain perspective.

Bonino's concept of 'double location' will be further developed and applied to our concerns with the manner in which theology might furnish a critique of sociological methods, assumptions, values and conclusions. Moving beyond the strictly epistemological concerns of social location, I wish first to make the point that different social contexts impact in different ways upon the theologian's engagement with sociology. For example, the contrasting milieux of Europe and Latin America have led to contrasting encounters with dialectical thought. Whereas in Europe once fervent proponents of the dialectical method have since tired of this approach, Latin

American liberation theologians continue to utilize key elements of such thought (Dussel, 1993, pp. 85–92). This difference in approach has its roots, I believe, in the contrasting reasons for which a Marxist social critique was first engaged.

Faced with the growing success of Marxist thought among the intellectual avant-garde of Europe (Kruks, 1990, pp. 14–16), it was assumed by many theologians that the hegemonic syntax of the dialectical method would have to be utilized if any theological apologetic to post-war society were to succeed. Furthermore, in seeking to establish an acceptable *raison d'être* for Christianity, theologians felt obliged to engage head-on Marx's dictum that truth is found only in and through an activity directed to the transformation of society (McLellan, 1977, p. 156). As such, European theologians set about establishing the *practical* relevance of the Christian faith in post-war Europe by constructing a theological argument in which the theoretical lacunae of traditional theology were filled with a variety of dialectical formulations, concepts and phrases (Fierro, 1977, pp. 76–126). For the European theological community, attention to practice was thereby subordinated to broader theoretical ends.

In sharp contrast to the European context, liberation theology's encounter with Marxist thought emerged directly from the practical concern to comprehend the prevailing conditions of poverty, exploitation and oppression at the base of Latin American society. Initial encounters with dialectical thought thereby comprised part of a broad-sweeping eclectic quest to find the most appropriate and fruitful theoretical tools to undertake the task of socio-analytical mediation (Andrade, 1991, pp. 36–51), a theoretical engagement born of practical necessity. Though initially lacking the theoretical finesse with which European theologians first engaged Marxist thought, the progressive deterioration of conditions at the base have served only to convince liberation theologians of the continuing validity of dialectical thought.

Situated within a certain position along the broad theological spectrum, different theologians look upon society through a wide variety of theoretical lenses; all of which inevitably impress themselves upon any resulting theological evaluation of the social realm. Working with a strong and well-defined notion of divine providence, for example, theologians utilizing the Lutheran concepts of 'orders' or 'mandates' come to the social sphere with an already normative view of the defining characteristics of a well-structured society. As such, society is adjudged healthy or ailing to the extent that due respect and support is accorded by its citizens to the divinely ordained structures of the family, political authority and the church (for example, Brunner, 1937, pp. 340–83; Bonhoeffer, 1955, pp. 252–67). The delimited nature of the social commentary evinced by such a perspective stands in contrast, for example, to that permitted by the differing understanding of divine providence utilized within process thought. Rejecting or modifying traditional metaphysical assumptions concerning God's attributes and action in the world, process thought articulates a distinctive picture of the Divine's creative ordering of the cosmos. As God does not (and, at times, cannot) approach the world with a pre-set agenda or given list of specific structures to be realized, there exists no detailed *a priori* theological critique upon which process thought might construct a social commentary. That which God seeks to realize is that which is the best for all, *given the circumstances*. The inductive nature of the process method thereby undercuts the formulation of any normative approach to the social sphere. Thus, a fundamentally different theological evaluation of matters pertaining to the family, state and church are permitted; with issues such as homosexuality, one-parent families and political dissent being treated in a contrasting manner (for example, Cobb, 1982, pp. 44–64). Although the vague and diffident manner in which sociological method is employed by Brunner and Bonhoeffer makes any further comparison difficult, it can nevertheless be posited that different theological starting points lead to different expectations and evaluations of the social sphere. This, in turn, engenders a differing *elective affinity* between the theological paradigm in question and the sociological methods, assumptions, values, and conclusions favoured by that paradigm.

The implications of the concept of double location for a critique of sociological methods, assumptions, values and conclusions gives rise to a certain paradox in the manner by which this critique is best effected. If theology is to offer the sociological community any constructive and consistent critique, it must first take account of the extent to which the double location of the theologian impacts upon the resultant theological product itself. Consequently, theology must seek to appreciate more fully the manner in which the theologian's social context and theoretical paradigm furnish the conditions of possibility within which theological reflection takes place. Such can only be done properly, however, with recourse to the epistemological insights and analytical findings of the social sciences. The *critiqued* thereby furnishes the critic with the means to its own critique!

The recognition of the paradoxical relationship which theology has with the social sciences does not, let it be stressed, lead to an impasse in any theological critique of sociology. Rather, it is the acceptance of the positive contribution which the social sciences offer theology in aid of a better under-standing of those empirical and theoretical processes which eventuate in the theological product. This having been said, the sociological product is constituted as much by its double location as is the theological product. Neither comes to the other with absolute objectivity, methodological neutrality or value-free aspirations (Milbank, 1990, pp. 101–43).

The heuristic service which sociology offers to theology cannot therefore be utilized without due caution, if not explicit hermeneutical suspicion. This suspicion, however, need not be grounded on a pessimistic fear of unbounded relativism. While the concept of double location highlights the *situated* nature of both theological and sociological reflection, it also emphasizes for the theological community the very means by which it is to effect its critique of the sociological endeavour. The means pointed up by an acceptance of double location is itself the very *location* from and within which theological reflection takes place. In acknowledging that theology is at all times a theology-in-context, the concept of double location overcomes method-ological nihilism by underlining the given *locus theologicus* as the fountainhead from which the whole theological enterprise emerges. It is in celebrating, rather than denying, its contextual nature that theology gains ready access to the very source material upon and from which it can launch a critique of sociological methods, assumptions, values and conclusions.

Andrew Dawson

The way forward

Defining theology as 'second order reflection' upon first-order experience, Fiorenza (1993, p. 254) highlights the umbilical link which any theology has with its given constituency. As a systematic articulation of lived experience, theology undertakes its task by first orientating itself to the particular community from which it springs. Utilizing the dominant narratives through which lived experience is collectively expressed, theologians gain access to the life-world of their contemporary community; a life-world constituted by a host of mutually dependent and interpenetrative values, assumptions, prejudices, aspirations and preoccupations (see Davis, 1994, pp. 96–111). In reflecting on these factors, the theologian is able to understand more clearly the key components by which first-order community experience is directed. Ordering these evaluative components in as systematic a fashion as the material will allow, theology is thereby furnished with the means to effect a critique of sociology and its findings. Permit me an example.

Faced with waning ecclesiastical influence in the political sphere, declining formal church attendance and decreasing religious discourse in the public domain, the sociological theme of secularization is said to be all but complete within contemporary Europe. Given the wealth of empirical indicators, religion is assumed to be losing hold on the modern psyche (for example, Wilson, 1966, 1976, 1982). Reflecting on a faith community in which the feeling of dependence on and orientation towards something other than ourselves remains to the fore, however, many theologians may regard the processes of secularization as anything but the all-embracing phenomenon of particular sociological representations. Martin (1969, 1978) and Bellah (1976) offer sociological attacks upon the secularization thesis along similar lines. While not calling into question the accuracy of certain empirical indicators, the vitality of a transcendent value-system within one's own community may well lead the theologian to ask questions about what exactly is being measured and the appropriateness of defining religiosity by means of institutional participation and elective vocabulary.

Even prior to engaging the secularization issue with any

theistic premise, the theologian with an eye to the context of theological reflection will be forced to ask questions of a more overt sociological relevance. Given the vibrancy of transcendent experience within my community ethos, does secularization comprise the disappearance of religiosity *per se*, or rather its mutation into less homogeneous and empirically verifiable forms? In short, so long as theologians remain focused on the discourse and experience of their own community, secularization is seen less as a proven thesis and more as a chimera-like creation. The secularization thesis does not measure the displacement of religion, but serves only to mask the inability of instrumental reason to entertain any divergent mind-set of a transcendent orientation. The theological critique of the sociological realm issuing from the above is this: cease trying to quantify the decline of religion within modern European society. Instead, seek to develop fresh approaches to appreciating the manner and extent to which religion has changed in content and expression during its contemporary submergence within modern secular reason. Only in such a way will the sociological community prepare itself for a fuller understanding of the role of religion within the postmodern era.

In line with the postmodern critique of Enlightenment rationality, the concept of double location encourages the celebration, rather than the traditional denigration, of the *situated* nature of theological reflection. It is, after all, this situation which provides the theologian with the content for and impetus towards an engagement with contemporary society and sociological theory, as our dealings with the secularization thesis have shown. In addition, the concept of double location enables theology to stave off any move towards a totalization of its own discourse. Now, the theologian can freely admit that 'theology is not absolute discourse. It is discourse *of* the Absolute' (Boff, 1987, p. 45). Eschewing the agenda of religious imperialism, the concept of double location further permits the ready acknowledgement of the boundaries of any given context.

At the same time, however, the concept of double location need not be supposed to result in that antifoundationalist relativism for which 'strong postmodernist' thinkers such as Jacques Derrida have become renowned (see also Guarino, 1996, pp. 654–89). In addition to forcing the theologian to take

Andrew Dawson

account of the manner and extent to which received tradition
sets the parameters to theological reflection, double location
further posits tradition as a community-based discourse, the
content of which can only be understood in relation to those
terms, concepts, preoccupations and methods it has borrowed
from society at large. As D. Z. Phillips (1971, pp. 134–5) has
made plain, there is no such thing as a self-contained,
hermetically sealed language game. In so regarding theological
reflection as *both* a tradition-formed, community-based
narrative *and* a socially constituted, hence publicly accountable
discourse, the concept of double location furnishes a dialectical
understanding of the relationship between theological reflection and sociological method. On the one hand, theology must
never cease to acknowledge that it is, at all times, a tradition-
led enquiry; and that it is this tradition which is the wellspring
of its critique of sociological methods, assumptions, values and
conclusions. Yet, on the other hand, as a socially founded and
publicly constituted discourse, theology must have constant
recourse to the social sciences, not simply as a means to a self-
critical consciousness but also (more importantly?) as a tool by
which the social fund from which theology draws its content
might be acknowledged and utilized as an epistemological
bridge by which one community-based tradition might engage
with others beyond its immediate boundaries. In effect,
theology needs sociology as much as sociology needs theology.

References

Andrade, P. F. C. (1991), *Fé e Eficácia: O uso da sociologia na
teologia da libertação*, São Paulo, Edições Paulinas.
Bellah, R. N. (1976), New religious consciousness and the crisis in
modernity, in C.Y. Glock and R. N. Bellah (eds), *The New
Religious Consciousness*, pp. 77–92, Berkeley, University of
California Press.
Boff, C. (1987), *Theology and Praxis: Epistemological Foundations*,
New York, Orbis.
Bonhoeffer, D. (1955), *Ethics*, London, SCM Press.
Bonino, J. M. (1983), *Toward a Christian Political Ethics*, London,
SCM Press.
Brunner, E. (1937), *The Divine Imperative*, London, Lutterworth.
Cobb, J. B. (1982), *Process Theology as Political Theology*,
Manchester, Manchester University Press.

Davis, C. (1994), *Religion in the Making: Essays in Social Theology*, Cambridge, Cambridge University Press.

Dussel, E. (1993), Theology of liberation and Marxism, in I. Ellacuría and J. Sobrino (eds), *Mysterium Liberationis: Fundamental Concepts of Liberation Theology*, pp. 85–102, New York, Orbis.

Fierro, A. (1977), *The Militant Gospel: An Analysis of Contemporary Political Theologies*, London, SCM Press.

Fiorenza, E. S. (1993), *Discipleship of Equals: A Critical Feminist Ekklesia-logy of Liberation*, London, SCM Press.

Guarino, T. (1996), Postmodernity and five fundamental theological issues, *Theological Studies*, 57, 654–89.

Kruks, S. (1990), *Situation and Human Existence: Freedom, Subjectivity and Society*, London, Unwin Hyman.

Kuhn, T. (1962), *The Structure of Scientific Revolutions*, Chicago, University of Chicago Press.

Libânio, J. B. (1991), *Teología de la Liberación: guía didáctica para un estudio*, Buenos Aires, Ediciones Paulinas.

McLellan, D. (1977), *Karl Marx, Selected Writings*, Oxford, Oxford University Press.

Mannheim, K. (1952), *Essays on the Sociology of Knowledge*, New York, Oxford University Press.

Martin, D. (1969), *The Religious and the Secular: Studies in Secularization*, London, Routledge.

Martin, D. (1978), *A General Theory of Secularization*, Oxford, Blackwell.

Milbank, J. (1990), *Theology and Social Theory: Beyond Secular Reason*, Oxford, Blackwell.

Phillips, D. Z. (1971), Religious beliefs and language games, in B. Mitchell (ed.), *Oxford Readings in Philosophy: The Philosophy of Religion*, pp. 121–42, Oxford, Oxford University Press.

Tillich, P. (1951), *The Protestant Era*, London, Nisbet & Co.

Wilson, B. (1966), *Religion in Secular Society: A Sociological Comment*, London, Pelican.

Wilson, B. (1976), *Contemporary Transformations of Religion*, Oxford, Oxford University Press.

Wilson, B. (1982), *Religion in Sociological Perspective*, Oxford, Oxford University Press.

4

Social Theories of the Human Agent and Monastic Dialogue

Jeff Vass

Introduction

S ociology in the twentieth century has tended theoretically to separate the activity of the human agent from larger 'contextual' forces (economy, ideology, social institutions) in order better to express either how the latter determines the former or how the agent constructs or makes the larger social world around her/him. Religion, since Durkheim and Marx, has been conceived as a 'macro-social' artefact which serves to co-ordinate the activities of human beings. In the tradition of Weber religion is viewed as a 'constructed outcome' of the interactivity of human agents; that is, through their endeavours to make sense of the world around them. Indeed, in *The Protestant Ethic and the Spirit of Capitalism*, Weber (1930) attempted to demonstrate how capitalism in its modern form could be shown to be the constructed outcome of the social and economic interactivity of human beings (Calvinists) whose behaviour is motivated by religious 'sense-making strategies'. Weber linked religious motivation in the Calvinist context to modes of interpretation. Calvinists read, interpreted and made sense of their world through the economic returns it produced. Weber is to be distinguished from Marx and Durkheim in that he proposes that the logic of belief supports the human agent's acts of constructing the social world by interpreting and unravelling the contingent circumstances of life. In any event

Weber is partly responsible for proposing a 'hermeneutical gap' between the world as 'book' and the human agent as 'reader'.

The issues of agency and social constructionism have to do with how human subjects *make* their social worlds, and make them *cohere* in ways which provide for the subsequent elaboration of human life. Fundamental to such a definition in the modern world are the freedoms and strategies of making and of coherence that have to do with interpreting and organizing the social world around us. 'Coherence', unlike 'making', is a word not usually found in this context. We are aware, and sociology celebrates this idea, that the social world is continually made around us: we construct it and it constructs us. What this picture fails to underline is that such making is undertaken in an uncertain context of historical contingency. History 'befalls' us.

Human agency traditionally involves social 'acts of making' or 'construction', and includes linguistic acts such as conversation and dialogue: but contemporary social theories tend to remove human authorship since historical forces are seen as having their own dynamic. With an emphasis on the latter, human activity has come to be seen more as an act of 'reading' rather than 'authoring'. My contention, then, is that ontological freedom has passed in sociology from being a condition of authorship to the uncertainties of our readership in the social world. Social consciousness and critique is about reading and interpreting representations of the world divorced from authorship. With this move the relations of human beings to each other, their social worlds and their own acts of making, now entail the transformation of an original freedom into an ontology of cynicism, suspicion or calculativeness. The monastic theology of dialogue, I argue, still provides an *alternative* theoretical resource to this sociology of human construction. Readership in monastic theology was never removed from the pedagogical context of 'conversation and conversion'. Authorship and readership were never divorced from one another theoretically. Whatever the historical realities of monastic life in the past or the present, this theoretical resource remains and stands as a critique of the perspective and inclination of social theory.

Contemporary social theories

Social theories seek to understand how social order arises and persists within human cultures. Formally they seek to describe the complex arrangement of activities and institutions that seem to comprise this order and determine its character and shape. Latterly structuralist and Weberian approaches to social order have focused on language, used as a powerful medium of oppression (rather than expression), which acts determinatively on the human agent. It should be understood that language is conceived here as a medium of social organization. In recent social theory (for example, Shotter, 1993; Giddens, 1979, 1981) language as a symbolic practice is an instrument of 'social making' before it is a means for representing our circumstances. However, there is a difference between those who focus on 'making' and those who focus on the 'already-made'. Shotter, for example, has emphasized the grammatical present of making while many critical sociologists emphasize the structuring properties of the world-as-already-made. Social theory tends towards the latter viewpoint especially when in critical mode (Bhaskar, 1989). It sees language as a symbolic activity that takes its place with other macrosocial processes such as economic and political processes. The gap between agent and 'social order' is a long-standing theoretical problem. It is the way in which sociology and theology understand this gap that perhaps best describes their theoretical distance. The distance between monastic theology and social theory most clearly reflects our problems concerning this gap.

Contemporary social theory tends to find the 'mood' of contemporary humanity in its cultural and political awareness of itself in relation to this 'gap' between agent and social order. We have arrived at views of human subjects which characterize us as ontologically cynical, or suspicious or calculative with respect to our 'ordered' social worlds and even our own acts of making. I want to suggest here that sociology is justified in providing a critical viewpoint for the oppressive conditions of modern humanity, but in so doing it has confused an ontology of society with a critique of society. Furthermore, in theorizing the relation between agent and society it has divorced activities of 'authorship' from 'readership' in our understanding of how humans act. This divorce has led to the various pessimisms concerning the human agent alluded to above. I now briefly trace the background to the gap in question.

The social 'order' of the nineteenth century appeared to Marx, Weber and Durkheim as if in a state of 'dislocation' from the human being upon whose agency it depended for its continuance. The nature of this dislocation was different for each theorist. For Marx it arose through the processes by which, under the conditions of capitalism, people become 'alienated' from what they produce. The meaning and value of these products arise from a system of values beyond the influence of the agent because they exist only within social and economic exchange. Furthermore, the agent becomes alienated from his/her own self because selfhood, in Marxian thought, is intimately connected with making and the fate of what one makes. For Durkheim social life hangs together through the commitments we make to social norms and the social strategies through which alignments to consensus are regulated. Durkheim saw the late nineteenth century as a period of rapid social change which made the job of orienting oneself to norms difficult: a sense of 'rule-lessness', anomie, follows. Weber focused on the rationalization of the agent's activities and the consequent 'disenchantment'. The control and guidance of social life no longer arose from custom, religious values or debated values grounded in long-held traditions, but from the cold and rational development of instrumental means to achieve technological ends.

Contemporary social theory about agency has developed from one or some of these founding positions. In twentieth century thought we have seen functionalism, structuralism, existentialism, psychoanalysis, feminism and latterly post-structuralism and postmodernism allying or engaging with these foundational statements. We can still detect their presence as social theorists attempt to outline why we experience the contemporary world in the dislocated way we do, and in attempting to say what the modern world, and living in it is like. Since the 1980s post-structuralist views have held centre-stage together with alliances with psychoanalysis and feminism. Structuralism itself, from the 1950s onward, had revolutionized our understanding of the connectedness of human agents to the social worlds that embed them. In fact, the agent vanished from view and became totally absorbed into matrices of structural determinations. Coward and Ellis (1977) famously wrote of the human agent as a locally determined 'fixity' amid numerous linguistic, psychological and social 'structures'. By the end of the 1970s many theorists were celebrating 'the death of the author'. The human subject could no longer be seen as the origin of activity. In many ways the agent was seen as incidental to the activities that constituted the social world and agency had become totally absorbed into social media.

The rise of social theory after structuralism attempted to regain a notion of the agent, if only as a partial, shadowy after-image of social process. Post-structuralism was as critical of the ontology of social systems as it was of any human essence forming the basis of human being. But the recent focus of social theory is still the question of the dislocated set of social forms that in some way construct the human as a particular kind of subject. These social forms are thought of as woven together as texts that give rise to 'representations'. Our common social worlds appear to consist of numerous stories and media forms which, through our active engagement with them, organize for us what kind of subjects we can potentially become. Structured into these representations are the social positions we may potentially take and from which we 'make'.

Who I am is manufactured from a process of engagement with representations which we may call 'reading'. Representations are ideological material and therefore are shared with other social agents. In critical mode we understand that the social distribution of power and opportunity is unfairly structured into these representations. Our activities take us through many different regions of our social world: lectures, parties, pubs, churches, courtrooms, surgeries and sweet shops. Each region brings together representational material from which we derive our subjectivity through acts of reading. Social construction and the makings of human action are now to be seen as the *coherence* that can be introduced to a set of heterogeneous texts.

Religion, like advertising, is seen as a source of representations from which agents derive their subjectivity through acts of reading. Via the process of reading agents are further constructed into relationships of power. Just as the power to define femininity lies with the advertising media drawing on numerous textual constructions of the feminine, so the power to define Christian personhood lies in the textual engagement of church with its secular context. 'Goodness' becomes a process of monitoring, according to textual criteria, the coherence that can be made by agents between church and other regions of their social world.

While there is much of *critical* importance in contemporary social theory of this kind, there are several problems which I would highlight for attention.

First, the divorce of reader from text entails an over-emphasis on how we 'read' the social world, its meanings and its 'representations'. Human discourse is seen as representational material which is already highly structured. The sense of human agency as a specifying and 'counter-specifying' force is lost from view. Contemporary theory has taken the dislocative effect that Marx envisaged had occurred between agent and networks of social value but has lost the alienated *agent*. Instead we now have the distance between *subject* and text constituted as an ontological 'cynicism'.

Second, the freedom and dynamic of human agency has been absorbed into representational texts: 'agency' has become the 'mobility' of texts. Human agents constitute the 'intertextuality' of these ideological formations, that is, that they interpenetrate one another. While the development of the constructionist viewpoint on human identity through discourse derives from Weber's foundational work, what is lost is the sense of historical process through which agents 'orientate' themselves towards the meanings that others make around them.

Third, there has been a collapse of the distinction between formal descriptions of representations/subjectivity and the critical discourse which needs to respect the ethical and political parameters of the human agent. Representationalism absorbed human agency partly because it wanted to suggest that, whatever we conceived human being as, it must always be a textual construction. For example, 'person' was a construction of Roman civic and legal discourses; and 'individual' was a construction of mid-eighteenth-century political and philosophical discourses. However, formal descriptions of representations cannot in themselves be critical. Currently simply asserting that some social circumstance or concept has been 'constructed' appears to serve as critical comment. But it is not clear why it should do so beyond the obvious that human circumstances are not given by nature. At least Marx had argued that human beings were in a condition of alienation from themselves because he retained an ontology of human being. Current theory relocates this ontology to the outcomes of the construction process. Hence, there can be no critical ethics of the processes of construction: and this is why ethics has become aesthetics or a matter of taste; because it is directed towards the objects that determine us as subjects.

Monastic dialogue and anti-representationalism

Contemporary social theories of human agency, whether originating from Marx, Weber or Durkheim, share with Christian theology a foundational belief in the human being's whole or partial freedom to make, construct, define or act otherwise than any current situation requires. For the Marxist tradition such freedom must always be a potential of reflective consciousness; for Durkheim it was expressed in how human beings aligned themselves to social rules and norms; and for Weber this basic freedom is necessary for what it is to construct and live in a rational social world. It is ironic that, as we have seen, a freedom basic to human being should give rise to its own total subjection to dislocated forces in modernity. I have discussed views of the human subject as something constructed from 'dislocated' texts: representations. In what follows I demonstrate, first, that representational theory is an unintended by-product of secularization and, second, that monastic theology retained an agent-centred ontology of dialogue language practices.

During the patristic era Christian theology gave a foundational place to a necessary freedom of human agency such that it became an ontological condition of being human with a potential for salvation (Zizioulas, 1985). During the post-patristic development of Western Christian monasticism, this principle can be seen as foundational to the educational arrangements made for the 'formation' of souls. Monasteries in the Benedictine tradition are 'schools of divine service' where monks undergo a lifelong pedagogical regime. This regime is 'dialogic' in character and depends on a 'conversation of conversion' (*conversio morum*). Monastic commitment to a dialogical conversion, whatever the realities in practice, provided for a theology of language, hermeneutics and historical contingency (Leclercq, 1982). Sociology inherited this provision long after it had infiltrated theology, Christian practice, philosophy and other secular learning.

The conversational view of dialogue situates acts of reading and interpreting within the *conversio morum* (conversion of customary practices). Responsiveness to history and meaning does not consist just in human beings becoming 'subject to' the representations and discourses that are manufactured impersonally, and unintentionally, around them. An ethical, personal and situational ideal had its origins in early monastic statutes and commentaries about communication and pedagogy in the monastic curriculum. These debates were themselves predicated on patristic thought. Monastic dialogism may be seen as a microcosm of Christian ideals but a microcosm which, of course, needs application to a greater variety of human contexts.

In brief, the secularization of interpreting, reading and pedagogical dialogue may be described in the following way. We start with an agent-centred, historically open practice of dialogic learning in pre-twelfth-century monastic schools. By the end of the fifteenth century dialogistic 'sense-making strategies' had been appropriated into a new rational form which sees the world itself as an 'order' which contains already-specified logical relationships available to mental and rational enquiry. The basis of contemporary sociological theories of representation arose from this appropriative move. Human agency, its freedom and need to make coherent action had passed from an ontological condition of human being to becoming a theoretical feature of the world, the *context* of action. This appropriative move was a silent one and has, I believe, not been acknowledged as the source of contemporary contradictions in social theory.

Although it took several hundred years to produce a silent 'dislocation' between agent and world, there had been a noisy debate on this very issue between Bernard of Clairvaux and Peter Abelard in the twelfth century. Bernard was a Cistercian monk who vehemently argued the necessity of *fides quaerens intellectum*: faith seeking wisdom. Abelard, however, famously argued that truth is discovered via a technology: Aristotelian logic. My concern is not with who was right, but with the social consequences of Abelard winning this debate in the sense that the 'secular' cathedral schools took up his version of dialectics rather than continuing with Bernard's traditional form of 'hermeneutical apprenticeship'.

The consequences of following Abelard's dialectics have serious implications for how, as 'truth-seeking beings', we make and lend coherence to our circumstances. Volosinov (1973) argued that secular dialectics proposed a 'radical objectivity' to sense-making. Human speech could begin to be thought of as a kind of output which had the same relation to speaker as hearers. That is, first- and second-person dialogue came to have a textual, third-person nature, for all participants, whose authority could be related only to the already-coherent arrangement of world or context. This is now referred to as the principle of 'ergodicity', namely that the world already contains logical relationships prior to acts of human construction. Monastic theology continued to resist, for a time, this ergodic authority for the guidance of acts of human coherence. Instead, monastic teachings continued to argue the notion that human sense-making must, to some extent, produce its own locally contingent grounds for the guidance of making and coherence. In this respect monastic teaching is 'anti-representational' both ontologically and critically: that is to say, we are not entirely subject to ergodic contexts, because we necessarily reflexively search for the freedom to ground our own dialogic activity. This reflexivity is central to patristic definitions of ontological freedom enshrined in monastic statutes. It is what has been lost in social theory and to which, from its 'dislocated' vantage point, it now seeks to return.

References

Bhaskar, R. (1989), *Reclaiming Reality: A Critical Introduction to Contemporary Philosophy*, London, Verso.

Coward, R. and Ellis, J. (1977), *Language and Materialism*, London, Routledge & Kegan Paul.

Giddens, A. (1979), *Central Problems in Social Theory*, London, Macmillan.

Giddens, A. (1981), *A Contemporary Critique of Historical Materialism*, London, Macmillan.

Leclercq, J. (1982), *The Love of Learning and the Desire for God: A*

Study of Monastic Culture, New York, Fordham University Press.
Shotter, J. (1993), *Conversational Realities: Constructing Life through Language*, London, Sage.
Volosinov, V. (1973), *Marxism and the Philosophy of Language*, Cambridge, Massachusetts, Harvard University Press.
Weber, M. (1930), *The Protestant Ethic and the Spirit of Capitalism*, London, Allen and Unwin.
Zizioulas, J. (1985), *Being as Communion*, London, Darton, Longman & Todd.

5

The Problem of Charismatic Religious Experience for the Sociology of Religion: Label or Libel?

Martyn Percy

Introduction

Most of us at one time or another have eaten baked beans. But how would you describe what you have eaten? For some, this is a convenient snack food. For others, it is an essential component in a child's meal. Still for others it is a rich source of protein, high in fibre and containing essential vitamins and minerals. In supermarkets, its marketing 'position' is quite different from what it might be in a health food shop. We know the product represents different things to different people. Few people, however, are likely to describe a tin of baked beans as this: 'beans (probably *Soja hispida*) baked in a liquid suspension consisting of water, sugar, salt, modified cornflour, spirit vinegar, vitamin B, spices and mono-emulsifiers'. Whilst this is an accurate narration of the contents of a tin of baked beans, many consumers would consider it peculiar to refer to the food in this way. They might wonder if it were more of a libel than a label. The descriptive aspirations tell us nothing about the experience of eating baked beans, and what is to be enjoyed about it.

The sociology of religion is, in part, an attempt at

categorization, 'establishing normative epochs' for meaning (D'Costa, 1996). It concerns itself with describing phenomena in common-sensical ways, creating categories of meaning and knowledge in order to give a 'social' account of what it sees. Thus, 'religion' tends to be treated like a 'thing', an 'object' of scientific analysis, and deconstructed accordingly. Correspondingly, religion is broken down into its (alleged) constituent parts (for example, sacred–profane), or referred to in functional terms (for example, 'social legitimization', 'projection'). Like many modernist human sciences however, it often fails to see *itself* as a construction of reality, social or otherwise. As Catherine Bell (1996, p. 188) points out: 'That we construct "religion" and "science" is not the main problem: that we forget we have constructed them in our own image – that is a problem.' In saying this, Bell is suggesting that a 'pure' description of phenomena is not possible. Both the human sciences and theology are engaged in an interpretative task, and describe what they see according to the prescribed rules of their grammar of assent. In the case of the sociology of religion, this has often tended to assume a humanist-orientated perspective, which has sometimes imagined itself to be 'neutral'. Thus, sociologists describe what they see, whilst theologians and religious people are said to 'ascribe' meaning to the same phenomena. On the other hand, those who have had religious experiences feel that what they experience is 'real', and the sociological account is therefore deemed to be at best complementary and at worst unrepresentative. Invariably, both approaches forget that 'religion' is something of a complex word with no agreed or specific definition. The dilemma between labelling and libelling lies here.

The genesis of the problem lies in nineteenth-century approaches to religion. Marx and Feuerbach, amongst others, distinguished between 'essence' and 'manifestation' in religion. Social, moral and scientific critiques of religion tended to see religion as a 'thing' that could be explained (away) in terms of the applied point of reference. For Durkheim (1965, p. 62), religion was 'a unified set of beliefs relative to sacred things'. For Marx (1844), it was 'the opium of the people' – the self-conscious, self-feeling of alienated humanity. For Freud (1939, p. 160), it was dreams and primal rites that became religious rituals. As Lash (1996) points out, these narratives of religion all have their place, but in what way do they correspond to the reality in which people find themselves? For example, if Marx, Durkheim and Freud all took a bus to their local church and advanced their theories on what was going on, how might believers respond? Very likely someone might turn to them and say: 'Oh no, love – you've got the wrong place. This is Church of England and Book of Common Prayer Matins. Have you tried up the road?'

Charismatic renewal?

In terms of charismatic religious experience, the problem is really quite sharp. A sociologist of religion sympathetic to the 'Toronto Blessing' wrote to me recently to suggest that whilst my work gave a careful ethnographic account of the movement, and had then applied a sociological discipline to the phenomenon ('the bones', as she put it), I had actually 'missed the soul' of the movement. My response was that sociology knew little of souls but was more concerned with structure – in this case, that of exchange (Percy, 1996b). Like Kipling's six blind men of Hindustan, each holding part of the elephant, I am prepared to agree that 'each are partly right'.

The problems that sociologists have in offering comprehensive accounts for human behaviour can be seen in John Elster's (1989) introductory work to the social sciences, from the point of view of rational choice theory. Although in many ways an exemplary work, offering theories for emotions, collective action and the like in terms of choice, the book serves as a typical example of a late modernist metanarrative. Without too much attention to ethnographic detail or exceptions to rules, the reader is offered a macro-theory of social life which, although illuminating, leaves much to be desired. Complex labelling of complex phenomena might be helpful, but social scientists have to be aware of the limitations, besides being conscious of the people such labelling serves. For example, does 'rational choice' really do justice to the compelling nature of a costly vocation? Equally, does an individualistic or collectivist account of human behaviour really explain the allure of a shrine for the pilgrim(s), or the non-rationality but controllability of speaking in tongues? In spite of Elster's best intentions and careful attention to method, the resultant theory still emerges as a kind of 'one size fits all' shoe – sometimes comfortable for some, but not always, and never for all.

According to Peter Winch (1958), a work like Elster's fails in its task because of the inadequate philosophical or epistemological basis that underpins the discipline. Critiques of sociology have been present since the 1950s, challenging the basis of rational accounts of the sublime (see Anscombe, 1957; Davidson, 1968), although the work of Winch is one of the more prescient in this respect, questioning the explanation and interpretation of human affairs in relation to social science. He argues that disciplines such as sociology fail to adequately comprehend the nature of intention and therefore the actual constitution of acts. This leads to a kind of false relativism, which might suit certain types of 'liberal' thinking but in fact does not assist us much in the task of finding the underlying truth or meaning of a belief system. More recently, John Milbank (1990) has critiqued the notion that there can be a 'social' vantage point from which to survey religion. He suggests that religion can always invert the relationship and deconstruct sociology, making it a faith; but Milbank only does this to attack the idea of a sociological 'metacritique', which he considers bogus, or at least something that should be significantly scaled down.

Following Milbank, I think that part of the problem is the assumed nature of relations in sociology: bi-polar, dialectical and essentially humanist. However, we should at least acknowledge the possibility of a ternary relationship, consisting objectively of the individual, society and God. This is why, when those within contemporary revivalism read the sociology of *their* religion, they often fail to recognize themselves, because 'God' has been ignored or reduced to a notion of projection or social legitimization. The theory does not correspond to their inner experience but only (just) to their ecclesial polity. This really will not do when it comes to interpreting the complex and rich nature of charismatic experience and religion, since the labels only make sense to those engaged in the business of social analysis: to the believers, it is just libel. That said, I believe that the sociology of religion still has a part to play in interpreting charismatic religion. Metacritiques have their uses; they are rather more like maps than close-up studies, a kind of ideological cartography, useful for charting complex data, but from a distance. Also, since ecclesial polity does reflect faith, it seems that sociology will always be in business when it comes to analysing belief systems. Notions of power, charisma, order can never be entirely monopolized by one discipline: their dynamics and language are always shared by theology, sociology and more besides.

To tackle a phenomenon like the 'Toronto Blessing' through a mainly sociological lens can only ever be an intermediate method in the hunt for authenticity and wisdom in matters of religion. Sociology, following its founding fathers such as Durkheim, Weber or Sohm, makes fundamental methodological presumptions about the nature of religion that not all religious believers will want to buy into. It assumes that religion is a human enterprise that can be described in humanistic terms, with reference to notions such as structure, ideology and sociality; that religion is a 'created' cosmos that brings stability, order, meaning and moral cement to a given community: the very word 'religion' means 'to bind', from the Latin. As such, considerable caution needs to be exercised by theologians who place sociology in the service of religious understanding, especially since some sociologists, such as Steve Bruce (1996) or Bryan Wilson (1970), sometimes seem to be setting themselves up as quasi-gurus, and their theories as secular alternatives or remedies to religion. Believing themselves to be 'neutral' (in the rather *passé*, modernist sense), it is almost as though they are preaching at times: 'Come to me, all ye who are religious, and I will explain.' Here, the sociology of religion emerges as a kind of 'Gnostic despair', in which scholars like Bruce lament the postmodern world in which 'choice' has broken down established religion. The sociology of religion therefore becomes a 'secret knowledge' in which agnostics can reorientate themselves in a universe of collapsing faiths (Bruce, 1996, p. 234).

Responses to this type of modernist metanarrative range from the crude to the sophisticated. Clearly, one such crude response is to engage in literalism or fundamentalist interpretation of experience, and distrust any serious analysis. Others may take the view that homogenizing data to fit a theory (for example, 'secularization') is actually just that, only sheltering under the umbrella of sociology. A presupposition about the decline of religion is likely to locate data that reinforces the point, but is that the right 'religious story' to be telling at the turn of the millennium? The Millennium, the New Age, Revivalism and 'popular piety' in the form of syncretic spirituality suggest a different narrative. As Grace Davie (1994) has suggested more subtly in respect of 'established' churches, not belonging does not necessarily imply not believing. More sophisticated, though, is the work of scholars like John Milbank, who trump the modernist metanarratives with a taste of their own medicine: his critique of the social sciences is a carefully constructed philosophy of suspicion turned back on to philosophies of suspicion. Others take a middle way. Scholars such as Kieran Flanagan (1996) are more selective in their adoption of sociological method, and clearly appreciate its capacity to illuminate religious studies, although they do not think it is the light, *per se*.

Sociology and theology

What, though, can theology gain from sociology? Obviously and principally, it is gaining a partner in dialogue that can enrich its self-understanding and help avoid the narcissism of 'interior enquiries' that are often uncritical and self-serving. Certainly, it cannot afford to assume that sociology is concerned with 'relationality', whilst theology is only to do with God. Ninian Smart's (1973, p. 10) claim that 'traditional theology has focused, naturally enough, on God as its subject-matter' misses the point that all theology is to do with that which *relates* to God – there are no 'pure' studies of God. Correspondingly, a consideration of charismatic religious experience cannot really afford to ignore the insights of sociologists such as Weber (1968), O'Dea (1963, 1983) or Percy (1996a, 1996b, 1997a, 1997b) on the nature of charisma itself. With reference to O'Dea (1963), a number of observations are pertinent.

There is no escaping the sociological dimensions that accompany charismatic renewal, 'Latter-Rain' and charismatic movements. No matter what *theological* story is being articulated in these groups, there is a *sociological* script to follow as well. O'Dea has identified 'five dilemmas of institutionalization' that affect charismatic movements. Each dilemma reflects a fundamental antinomy between charisma and the pressure to routinize it for the sake of the institution, so that religious experience is rendered continuously available for the masses to provide stability. The first dilemma concerns the status of the original message and the maintenance of its prescient power. Clearly, this places great emphasis on the original messenger, although postmodern revivalism apparently seems to be quite 'decentred' in this way. The second dilemma is over how the 'sacred' or the experience of the numinous is to be objectified and reified. Typically, this is done in the context of worship, ritual 'clinics' or in preaching. But in spite of the organization, perceptions remain highly subjective. A third dilemma arises directly out of this, namely assessment of the appropriate structures for inculcating charismatic experience: there will always be disagreements over how it is routinized, and the consequent hegemonic ecclesiology. This leads to a fourth dilemma: delimitation. Definitions of charismatic phenomena tend to 'kill the spirit', but some limits have to be placed on acceptable phenomena or the movement risks gross subjectivity and eventual relativity. Fifth, the exercise of power also poses a dilemma. 'Power language' is common to theology and sociology, and there is a great temptation in charismatic groups to conflate sacred and profane notions of power in order to protect 'the religion' itself.

I used exchange theory to elucidate the 'Toronto Blessing' (Percy, 1996b), and in so doing, attempted to demonstrate that the claim to experience the power of God *directly*, immediately and authoritatively requires a little more critical reflection. The rhetoric and religion of what I would dub 'unmediated zapping' is mesmerizing and magical; but it also results in rational abrogation. The human sciences can help us to see that claims on religious experience cannot be made and accepted in a simple, literalistic fashion. (Neither, of course, can they be rejected out of hand.) All religious experience is mediated through some agency or other, such as language, ideology, social or ecclesial structure. It is therefore open to some enquiry through social science. God is both present in and beyond sociality, so sociology and theology need each other here, if wisdom is being sought, not simply interpretation. In using the sociology of religion carefully, one is not engaged in the task of ultimate humanist reduction, whereby the power of God is always deemed to be a human projection. Rather, the enterprise is geared towards showing that any powers of God that might be known are often subtle, ambiguous and open to a variety of explications.

For example, accounts of 'miracles' are invariably interpretations of events, not simple, pure descriptions that require blind acceptance or naked rejection. 'Miracles' do happen, I am sure, just as God's power is real. But psychological, sociological, anthropological and phenomenological accounts of the same can complement, critique and illuminate the eyes of faith that may have seen the hand of God. Those who are for the 'Toronto Blessing' are actually engaged in the exercise of descriptive interpretation, as much as any sociologist of religion. The real issue is over the quality and form of rational-faith basis that constructs the explanation. Literalistic interpretations are typically still, framed, black and white portraits: social science can give colour, sound and movement to the same image, helping to convey the complexity of what is taking place. Neither ultimately monopolizes the truth to the exclusion of the other.

Thus, when put together, sociology and theology can learn from and enrich each other. Samuel Taylor Coleridge (1840, pp. 39–81) helpfully makes the distinction between *apprehension* (the rational-empirical) and *comprehension* (the religious imagination, historically aware and self-conscious) in the study of faith. In the context of late modernity or postmodernity, the journey from apprehension to comprehension in theology and religious studies needs to avoid the polarized dualisms of modernity, and requires (at times) a trusting synthesis of social science and theology (Hardy, 1996, pp. 305–27). This is especially the case when evaluating experience, ecclesiology, faith-claims and the like (Middlemiss, 1996).

When deliberately kept apart, the results can be rather odd. For example, Steve Bruce (1996, p. 10) identifies Christianity as a 'monotheistic' religion. This allows him to begin his thesis by making a general sociological point about systematic religion, rationalized worship, order, logic and stability. There are many sociologists who see the unity of communities in similarly modernist terms, as though unity somehow simply lay in social structure (for example, Suttles, 1972; Newby, 1980). Bruce (1996, p. 234) can then conclude the same thesis by pointing out how the one, universal 'thunderous symphony' has given way

Martyn Percy

to many different kinds of 'enthusiastic music makers', by which he means postmodernism. Ironically, were Bruce better informed about theology and about enthusiastic religion, his thesis would be much richer; but as it stands, he is just wrong. Christianity is neither monotheistic or polytheistic, but Trinitarian. Theologically, ecclesiologically and therefore sociologically, a degree of relational-plurality is implied in its ontology. The proliferation of enthusiastic, charismatic or revivalist sects and 'churches' can, in part, be traced to the absence of such a doctrine in their midst. Most of these groups are either non-Trinitarian or possess a warped doctrine, which then produces a dysfunctional ecclesiology, which has direct social consequences. Charismatic movements are not built on doctrine but on experience, created 'communities of feeling', and on charisma. They fall apart precisely because they prefer the simplicity of monotheism and subsequent ecclesial-monarchical government to the complexity of liberal relationality that is embedded in an articulated doctrine of the economic Trinity. Revivals are caught, not taught; they have little 'theological' basis (Percy, 1996a, 1997a, 1997b). Thus, if Bruce could see which theological components were missing in charismatic religion, he would have a better-informed sociological account of religious fissure and the rise of new schisms.

Conclusion

It would be wrong to suggest, however, that reductive accounts are necessarily damaging to faith. On the contrary, such accounts provide helpful skeletons that might suggest anything from a pathology to a cure. Theologians who are interested in studying religious movements cannot afford to ignore these insights. Whilst it is true that autopsies give no insight into the condition of the soul, they nonetheless tell us something about how a body lived and moved, and what might have eventually killed it. With respect to the use of something like exchange theory, it is true that it runs the risk of flirting with a Marxist, Non-Realist (theological) account of religious phenomena. Yet it can also be used in the service of simple social realism, which is surely a worthy theological goal. So far as the use of this or that theory goes, no one could or should suggest that it provides a *comprehensive* account of something like the

'Toronto Blessing'. Rather, it is a *complementary* account, which has the effect of challenging the claims made for the 'blessing'; in my view, this is a necessary component in the task of discernment, and for the pursuit of wisdom.

References

Anscombe, G. (1957), *Intention*, Oxford, Blackwell.

Bell, C. (1996), Modernism and postmodernism in the study of religion, *Religious Studies Review*, 3, 179–90.

Bruce, S. (1996), *Religion in the Modern World: From Cathedrals to Cults*, Oxford, Oxford University Press.

Coleridge, S. (1840), *Confessions of an Inquiring Spirit*, London, Taylor Hennesey.

Davidson, D. (1968), Actions, reasons and causes, in A. R. White (ed.), *The Philosophy of Action*, pp. 21–7, Oxford, Oxford University Press.

Davie, G. (1994), *Religion in Britain Since 1945: Believing without Belonging*, Oxford, Blackwell.

D'Costa, G. (1996), The end of 'theology' and 'religious studies'? *Theology*, 99, 338–51.

Durkheim, E. (1965), *The Elementary Forms of Religious Life*, New York, New York Free Press.

Elster, J. (1989), *Nuts and Bolts for the Social Sciences*, Cambridge, Cambridge University Press.

Flanagan, K. (1996), *The Enchantment of Sociology: A Study of Theology and Culture*, London, Macmillan.

Freud, S. (1939), *Moses and Monotheism*, New York, Vintage.

Hardy, D. (1996), *God's Ways with the World: Thinking and Practising Christian Faith*, Edinburgh, T. & T. Clark.

Lash, N. (1996), *The Beginning and End of Religion*, Cambridge, Cambridge University Press.

Marx, K. (1844), *On Religion*, Moscow, Foreign Languages Publishing.

Middlemiss, D. (1996), *Interpreting Charismatic Experience*, London, SCM Press.

Milbank, J. (1990), *Theology and Social Theory: Beyond Secular Reason*, Oxford, Blackwell.

Newby, H. (1980), *Community*, Milton Keynes, Open University.

O'Dea, T. (1963), Sociological dilemmas: five paradoxes of institutionalisation, in E. A. Tiryakian (ed.), *Sociological Theory, Values and Sociocultural Change: Essays in Honour of Pitirim A. Sorokin*, pp. 71–89, New York, Free Press of Glencoe.

O'Dea, T. (1983), *The Sociology of Religion*, Englewood Cliffs, New Jersey, Prentice Hall.

Percy, M. (1996a), *Words, Wonders and Power: Understanding Contemporary Christian Fundamentalism and Revivalism*, London, SPCK.

Percy, M. (1996b), *Catching the Fire: The Sociology of Exchange in the 'Toronto Blessing'*, Oxford, Latimer House.

Percy, M. (1997a), City on a Beach: neo-Pentecostalism at the turn of the millennium, in T. Walter and S. Hunt (eds), *Neo-Pentecostalism at the End of the Twentieth Century*, pp. 40–59, London, Macmillan.

Percy, M. (1997b), *Is there a Charismatic Theology?* Oxford, Farmington Institute.

Smart, N. (1973), *The Science of Religion and the Sociology of Knowledge*, Princeton, Princeton University Press.

Suttles, G. (1972), *The Social Construction of Community*, Chicago, Chicago University Press,.

Weber, M. (1968), *Charisma and Institution Building*, Chicago, Chicago University Press.

Wilson, B. R. (1970), *Rationality*, Oxford, Blackwell.

Winch, P. (1958), *The Idea of a Social Science*, London, Routledge.

6

Sociological Methodologies and the Changing Nature of Contemporary Fundamentalism

Stephen J. Hunt

Fundamentalism and worldly-accommodation

There has long been a recognition within the discipline itself that the sociology of religion is beset by numerous, almost insurmountable methodological difficulties. The tendency for sociology to carry its own rationalizing secularizing ethos (Martin, 1966), the way in which it has all too often insensitively dealt with subjective transcendental religious 'experiences' of the actor (Garrett, 1974), and the danger of taking sides with anti-cultist/sectarian sentiments (Lewis, 1987) are among the well-documented methodological issues.

Plainly, these problems relate to different religious groups and movements to varying degrees. As an over-simplified statement we might argue that the more 'fundamentalist' a group, the more these methodological difficulties appear in clear relief. Those which claim to hold a greater understanding of the 'truth' and who see themselves in tension with society do not lend themselves easily to academic research. No matter how finely tuned the sociological tools, no matter how critically aware researchers are of methodological shortcomings, there is something inherent in a world-view which appraises all in terms of black and white, good and bad, the godly and the satanic which breeds a profound mistrust of 'unsaved' secular humanists (Zaretsky and Leone, 1979, p. 12), not least of the sociological variety.

Christian fundamentalism has traditionally been interpreted as a negative reaction in theological and practical terms towards modernity and its secularizing impulses: rationalism, pluralism, subjectivism, and materialism (Hunter, 1981). It follows that it tends to carry an antagonism towards the outside world and fears, above all, compromise and accommodation with it (Ammerman, 1950, p. 4). The reality, however, is that fundamentalism rarely totally rejects what modernity has to offer since it indeed brings 'mixed blessings'. Hence, Ammerman (1950, p. 19) concedes that while fundamentalists are 'warriors against modernity' they may come to adopt beliefs and practices that are genuinely 'new' and correspond with cultural changes. It is apparent, therefore, that fundamentalists will utilize certain aspects of modern culture, usually for their own purposes, while rejecting others.

Pentecostalism is typical of this tendency. At first glance both classical and neo-Pentecostalism, with the emphasis upon the experience of the supernatural, the miraculous and the charismata, and a tendency towards millennialism, would appear to betoken a reaction against the forces of modernity particularly where they made incursions into the Christian Church (Martin, 1990, p. vii). Consequently, Pentecostalism has generally inclined to be sectarian in nature and displayed a prevailing tension with society. At the same time, however, it has always been culturally adaptive and its great accomplishment, at least within the context of Western societies, lies in its reaction to contemporary culture in that it can act against, but is simultaneously adaptive towards, modern trends (Cox, 1996). From a position of hindsight at the end of the twentieth century Pentecostalism appeared to be, in the words of Andrew Walker (1997), 'thoroughly modern' in that it had readily endorsed and positively embraced many aspects of the contemporary world.

At this point there needs to be some theoretical conjecture and it is one which unashamedly subscribes to the secularization thesis that, in the Western context at least, the authority and legitimacy of Christianity is undermined. In order to endure and engage with the world the long-term tendency is to compromise with it. Hence appraisals such as that of Hunter

(1987) argue that evangelical fundamentalism finds it increasingly difficult to sustain a thoroughgoing disapproval of the modern world. According to Hunter there has been, over time, a deliberate or unwitting accommodation by evangelicalism to its wider environment. Essentially, this has eased the tensions that necessarily exist because of the growing incongruities it has with modernity which allow participation in society with the minimum of cognitive dissonance. This does not mean that there are not enclaves of sectarian resistance but, by and large, worldly accommodation is the primary means of carving out a place for evangelicalism in the emerging world order (Hunter, 1987, p. 195–7).

The success of the Vineyard movement

Perhaps of all strands of neo-Pentecostalism the Vineyard organization most typifies some of these major trends and, indeed, they may explain its success. In the United States Vineyard has attracted academic interest precisely because it appeared to be the epitome of the thriving conservative/fundamentalist wing of Christianity (Perrin and Mauss, 1991). It has grown from its original independent fellowship in Anaheim, California, expanding rapidly to become a fully-fledged international movement: the Association of Vineyard Churches. At least 40 countries outside North America have Vineyard congregations with a total membership in the region of 50,000 people.

More recently, Vineyard has achieved a higher profile as the centre of that ecstatic and esoteric phenomenon which became popularly known as the 'Toronto Blessing'. Spread rapidly across the world, it impacted upon the various streams of neo-Pentecostalism from early 1994, characterized by such physical manifestations as uncontrollable laughter, shakings, twitching, 'spiritual drunkenness', and animal-like behaviour (Hunt, 1995).

There can be little doubt that in various ways Vineyard has made concessions to the contemporary world that appear to belie its fundamentalism. In fact, its success can be reduced to its ability to hold the balance between contemporary culture and elements of fundamentalism. Vineyard has articulated a belief system that is sufficiently all-embracing as to provide its membership with a sense of belonging to 'true' Christianity without the strictness and sense of obligation to the elect community traditionally associated with Christian fundament-alism (Perrin and Mauss, 1991).

Theologically speaking, Vineyard is one of the most vigorous expressions of the so-called 'Third Wave' movement which can be understood as a self-reflective and dynamic interpretation of the Christian Church at the end of the twentieth century. While not doing justice here to an elaborate theological construct, the principal teaching of the Third Wave is that all expressions of 'true' born-again Christianity, classical Pentecostalism, charis-matic renewal and traditional evangelicalism are being prepared for evangelism leading up to the Second Coming of Christ.

To this belief system John Wimber has made his own notable theological contribution: 'Kingdom Theology'. Wim-ber (1985) argued that while the Kingdom will be ushered in full with Christ's return it can, in some measure, be encountered now with supernatural phenomena if God is given room to act through the faith of believers. Here is the recurring theme of God dynamically intervening in history, of move-ments fostering the charismata, of demonstrative signs and wonders, and the conflict between the spiritual powers of good and evil.

Much of Wimber's theology is culled from that developed at Fuller seminary where he taught from 1975 to 1979 on church growth and evangelism. Part of the vision at Fuller appeared to be a thorough-going fundamentalism which vigorously at-tempted to reverse what was perceived as a damaging and counterproductive world-view derived from the Enlightenment which stripped modernity of much of its supernatural perceptions. The essential need was felt to be in rediscovering the 'experience' of the Christian faith and the reality of the supernatural.

While Vineyard's theological component constitutes an open challenge to the sceptical secular world there is, simultaneously, a set of rationally-orientated strategies embraced by the movement which is undoubtedly anchored in modernity. Again this reflected a number of theological threads woven at Fuller which attempted to bridge the gap between American fundamentalism and theological liberalism. While holding on

to unquestionable and fundamental 'truths', there was an attempt to make the gospel relevant to modern man and woman and hence advance the validity of the church. In attempting to combine these two divergent and apparently irreconcilable views Fuller, and later Vineyard, endorsed the best of what the modern world had to offer: secular methods of business and organizational growth and the utilization of the social sciences. However, the concession is a conditional one and the acceptability largely depends upon whether academic insights can be brought within and legitimize a fairly stringent world-view.

Fuller's School of World Mission produced the church-growth school of thought which argued that Christ's Great Commission of 'making disciples of all nations' (Matthew 38:16–20) was best achieved by sociologically examining successful churches, including the principles and dynamics behind their expansion. Among the teachings it espoused was that of the 'homogeneous unit principle'; that potential converts will be attracted to churches comprised of people of the same social background as themselves. This has been brought to the greatest fruition where Vineyard has provided a fundamentalist Christianity congruent with the life-styles of affluent middle-class 'baby-boomers' born in the United States during the 1960s: well-educated, career-minded and generally prosperous individuals. Taking much of its tone from the Jesus Movement of the early 1970s, Vineyard has diluted the 'counter-culture' into an attractive package for the middle-classes with a great deal of emphasis on casual dress, contemporary music and spontaneity in worship.

Sociology and psychology merged with theology in Wimber's 'Miraculous Church Growth' course at Fuller. This put into practice the work of such Christian psychologists as John White who had previously brought analytical science to focus upon human emotions and their relationship to the coming of the Holy Spirit in times of revival. His work stressed the consanguinity between fundamentalism and rational secularity since it attempted scientifically to account for the behavioural manifestations in the great revivals of the past including those of Wesley, Whitfield and Edwards. Religious revival, he argued, invokes strong emotions yet at the same time they may be psychologically and sociologically induced. In short, the

Holy Spirit brings signs and wonders, healings, miracles and other manifestations under specific conditions if people are open to them. For White (1987), the foremost consideration is in creating these psychological and sociological conditions which would allow the Spirit of God to work.

None of these cultural concessions, however, are sufficient to negate Vineyard's fundamentalist underpinnings. It is not without good reason that Martyn Percy (1996) largely focuses on Vineyard in his analysis of contemporary fundamentalist-revivalism. According to Percy, the distinguishing feature of fundamentalism is that believers perceive God working through them. Vineyard, in common with many strands of neo-Pentecostalism, sustains a self-referring theological system which sees itself, to use its own jargon, 'at the cutting edge' of what God is supposed to be doing in the Christian church. The emphasis may be more upon the unmediated experience of God's power rather than biblical literalism, but the fundamentalist principle remains; there is a fairly closed and uncompromising cognitive world-view.

Gateways into the Vineyard

The key question is how do movements such as Vineyard, which itself appears to react positively to the virtues of the social sciences, respond to the enquiries of academia itself? The answer is not so straightforward. Other issues have muddied the waters so that Vineyard is guarded towards outside scrutiny. The organization has spawned its own share of controversy. Spurious predictions of worldwide revival, as well as the scandal surrounding moral behaviour of some of its leaders, have taken their toll. The Toronto Blessing has also attracted its fair share of criticism.

Vineyard operates as an extensive organization run largely on business and bureaucratic lines. Interfacing with the public, media and academia is part and parcel of everyday church life. Hence, Vineyard exhibits many of the features of contemporary religious movements in that it is sufficiently prepared, at least at one level, to dialogue with the secular world. However, it does this largely within its own fundamentalist framework.

Previous academic studies of the Vineyard organization seem to have met with widespread acceptance and co-operation at

both the leadership and grassroots level. This was the case with Perrin's (1989) excellent large-scale research into the motivation and social background of Vineyard's members. Dismissing Wimber's claim that his churches were winning new converts, Perrin proved that the source of recruitment was, in fact, from other churches. This study, nevertheless, was fairly 'safe' in that it was largely uncritical of the Vineyard organization and relatively unobtrusive.

A second survey, by Margaret Poloma (1995), focused upon the Vineyard Toronto church which lent its name to the Toronto Blessing. Clearly, however, the survey was conducted with the co-operation of the Toronto church and appears to have been positively encouraged. While it is critical of John Wimber, it portrays the church in a favourable light. Focusing upon the beneficial effects of 'the Blessing' on those who made the pilgrimage to Toronto from different parts of the world, Poloma's research is, by any criteria, extremely sympathetic.

My own interest in the Vineyard organization was derived from a wider survey of neo-Pentecostalism and was principally concerned with accounting for its significant impact in Britain. Since the early 1980s, Vineyard's teachings and practices have reinvigorated charismatic renewal and brought to numerous churches the experience of neo-Pentecostalism for the first time. Because I was concerned with the motivation of its membership, the survey extended beyond interviews with the leadership to quantitative and qualitative research at congregational level.

Optimism about a similar positive response from the Vineyard organization in Britain was unfounded. Initial contact with the Vineyard hierarchy was met with a curt reply and ultimately a flat refusal to enter into dialogue. An early correspondence asked for copious details. What was the aim of my research? What was my personal motivation? What were the theological and sociological presuppositions that I held? Could I provide a summary of research I had previously undertaken on Vineyard? Why did I wish to study Vineyard's impact in Britain?

The correspondence also pointed out that Vineyard had been inundated by requests to be researched from both sociological and theological quarters. Consequently, it was deemed impractical to accommodate all of them and it was considered necessary to assess the benefit and impact of each request in terms of the likely investment of time that it would require from the Vineyard organization. Since Vineyard was allowing some research to be conducted, it was apparent that it was choosing what it regarded as important, relevant and indeed, desirable.

The failure of the organization's hierarchy to endorse research did not prevent work at a grassroots level within Vineyard congregations and on the movement's impact in the New Churches, Anglican and Baptist charismatic churches. Among the pastors of such churches, at least at the initial stages of research, there was a great deal of expressed desire for co-operation. This reflected a certain Christian charity of sorts. The stranger at the gate comes in different guises. Some were even flattered at the attention offered.

There was also, at one level, a very real recognition of the alleged benefits of sociology. Several pastors, in the course of conversation, produced a copy of Andrew Walker's (1985) theological and sociological work on the Restorationism movement. One pastor enquired 'What is Walker saying about us these days?' Some pastors even had a degree in sociology. The problem was that having some knowledge of the discipline only fuelled the speculation of some pastors that there was some sociological hidden agenda or, at the very least, there was the view that a sociological reduction would ultimately be a critical one. However, a few of those who agreed to a more detailed survey were attracted by the idea of using the findings about their church membership to increase the size of their congregations which, in neo-Pentecostal circles, is more or less an imperative.

Vineyard congregations and those inspired by Vineyard in Britain, like those in the United States, tend to be middle-class (but perhaps not quite so affluent). In some respects middle-class and educated members of religious movements have been noted as among the least co-operative when faced with academic research. The primary reason appears to be an informed view of the possibility of stigmatization and ridicule as a result of belonging to a 'deviant' religious group (Gerlack and Hine, 1976, p. 21). In my research experience this was only partly true and fear of criticism was tempered by an appreciation of what the social sciences could achieve. For instance, in an interview with a church member I was given a complex elucidation, not only of the problems facing the Christian in the postmodern world but also of the implications of postmodernist theory for academic research. In the same breath, however, he insisted that my own interest could not be purely academic since I had been led into Christian circles by God and that it was his responsibility to show the shortcomings of sociology and try to win me over to the faith.

A tale-ender: the Toronto Blessing

Many of the dilemmas in dealing with fundamentalist/ evangelical groups were evident with the arrival of the Toronto Blessing, along with some new ones. Although certain aspects of the physical phenomena associated with the 'Blessing' had been witnessed before in charismatic churches, their intensity took many seasoned charismatics as well as experienced observers of the movement by surprise. In the course of my research the 'Blessing' was an unfolding drama – advantageous in that it was the opportunity to study an ecstatic expression of Christianity first hand, but disadvantageous in that it raised acute methodological difficulties. At the very least it temporarily prevented the distribution of questionnaires and complicated interviews. It also indicated that such movements as that of the Third Wave may become increasingly unpredictable and inconsistent in their attitudes towards academic research.

The sociological explanations of the 'Blessing' vary considerably. It is clearly an extremely complex phenomenon. Such esoteric movements may mark an attempt to revive an increasingly beleaguered world-view in a world where there are few certainties. It might be seen as a kind of 'ghost dance' within Christianity, in other words, a nihilistic millenarian movement that is going nowhere in particular. At the very least it may show that in the future neo-Pentecostalism will be prone to ecstatic outbreaks for which the sociological methodologies are scarcely adequately prepared. The emphasis upon the charismata had always highlighted this within the movement. In the churches under study the personal experiences of the membership were often withheld because it was deemed to be beyond the grasp of social science. Divine revelations, especially through 'words of knowledge' or prophecy, were not open to academic scrutiny.

References

Ammerman, N. (1950), *Bible Believers: Fundamentalism in the Modern World*, London, Rutgers University Press.

Cox, H. (1996), *Fire from Heaven: The Rise of Pentecostal Spirituality and the Reshaping of Religion in the Twenty-first Century*, London, Cassell.

Garrett, W. (1974), Troublesome transcendence: the supernatural in the scientific study of religion, *Sociological Analysis*, 35, 169–80.

Gerlack, L. and Hine, V. (1976), *People, Power, Change: Movements of Social Transformation*, Indianapolis, The Bobbs Merril Co.

Hunt, S. (1995), The 'Toronto Blessing': a rumour of angels? *Journal of Contemporary Religion*, 10, 257–71.

Hunter, J. (1981), Operationalising evangelicalism: a review, critique and proposal, *Sociological Analysis*, 42, 36–72.

Hunter, J. (1987), *Evangelicalism: the coming generation*, Chicago, University of Chicago Press.

Lewis, J. (1987), The scholarship of 'cults' and the 'cult' of scholarship, *Dharma*, 12, 96–107.

Martin, D. (1966), Some utopian aspects of the concept of secularisation, *International Yearbook for the Sociology of Religion*, 2, 22–39.

Martin, D. (1990), *Tongues of Fire: The Explosion of Protestantism in Latin America*, Oxford, Blackwell.

Percy, M. (1996), *Words, Wonders and Power: Understanding Contemporary Christian Fundamentalism and Revivalism*, London, SPCK.

Perrin, R. (1989), *Signs and Wonders: The Growth of the Vineyard Fellowship*, Unpublished PhD dissertation, Washington, Washington State University.

Perrin, R. and Mauss, A. (1991), Strictly speaking ... Kelly's quandary and the Vineyard Christian Fellowship, *Journal of the Scientific Study of Religion*, 32, 125–35.

Poloma, M. (1995), *By Their Fruits: A Sociological Assessment of the Toronto Blessing*, Toronto, Toronto Airport Vineyard Church.

Walker, A. (1985), *Restoring the Kingdom: The Radical Christianity of the House Church Movement*, London, Hodder.

Walker, A. (1997), Thoroughly modern: sociological reflections on the Charismatic Movement from the end of the twentieth century, in S. Hunt, M. Hamilton and T. Walter (eds), *Charismatic Christianity: Sociological Perspectives*, pp. 17–42, London, Macmillan.

White, J. (1987), *Signs and Wonders Today: The Story of Fuller Theological Seminary's Remarkable Course on Spiritual Power*, Altamonte Springs, Florida, Creation House.

Wimber, J. (1985), *Power Evangelism: Signs and Wonders Today*, London, Hodder & Stoughton.
Zaretsky, I. and Leone, M. (1979), *Religious Movements in Contemporary America*, Princeton, Princeton University Press.

7

Sociology in Evangelical Theological Colleges

Tony Walter

Introduction

'It's only as a result of doing your course that I at last understand why I'm going into the Anglican ministry.' This comment was included in an ordinand's end-of-course evaluation after she had completed her 'Church and Society' option, taken in the eighth term of her nine-term BA in theology. How was it, I wondered, that a mere ten-week diet of Emile Durkheim, Max Weber, Peter Berger and Bryan Wilson had whetted her appetite for the ministry, whereas Old Testament, New Testament, Greek, Hebrew, systematic theology, church history and ethics had merely given her intellectual indigestion? Had she not opted for 'Church and Society', would she have been ordained without really knowing why? I was intrigued.

From 1986 to 1993, I taught the aforementioned course at Trinity Theological College, Bristol. This is an evangelical college, strongly influenced by the charismatic movement, and most of its students are preparing for the Anglican ministry. 'Church and Society' was an optional third-year course and proved one of the most popular. I have also taught a somewhat longer course, including a section on the psychology of religion, as a second-year option on the BA in theology at London Bible College, an independent non-denominational theological college which attracts Baptist, Anglican and other students intending to go on to a range of ministries in the church and in society, only a minority going on to the ordained ministry. The students in both colleges ranged from young twenties to late thirties, with an average age in the early thirties.

Teaching these students has been by far the most rewarding experience in my thirteen years of teaching at degree level, far more so than teaching on the BA in sociology in two mainline universities. Year in, year out, students evaluated my short and rather academic sociology course as the most relevant of their entire three-year theology degree. One student, writing several years later, contrasted my course with the rest of his BA: 'Relevance and stimulation have far too rarely been adjectives applicable to theological education.' In this chapter I explore why a sociologist should have found it so rewarding to teach committed Christian theological students, and why these students should have found the sociology of religion so stimulating, pertinent and challenging.

Why should sociology be part of theological training?

First, just as missionaries must understand the society to which they are being sent (necessitating anthropologically informed training), so clergy and other Christian workers in modern Britain need to understand the society to which they are to minister (Newbigin, 1989). This has been argued so often that it needs no further justification here, though much of this chapter describes how this can work out in pedagogical practice.

It just so happens that the major theories in the sociology of religion are pretty much the big theories in sociology. The role of religion and its decline is no sociological sideline but was crucial to the discipline's founding fathers. Students thereby encounter some of the formative thinkers of the modern world: Marx, Freud, Durkheim, Weber. This is most striking in the psychology of religion, where students gain a basic introduction to Freud, one of the most influential thinkers of the twentieth century. At the end of the course, students should have had their eyes opened not only to the modern social world, but also to the modern intellectual world.

Second, and possibly more important, sociology sees the church as a *social* institution. This perspective is particularly important for evangelicals and charismatics who tend to see their faith in highly individualistic terms. In addition, evangelicals can become so focused on the Bible that they end up with a weak understanding of the Church, while charismatics tend so to trust experience that they fail to look at the social and psychological processes that underlie experience. Because sociology is realistic about the churches to which such students belong and to which they are to devote the rest of their lives, they often find that the sociology of religion illuminates aspects of the Church with which they are familiar but about which they had not hitherto enquired sociologically.

Sociological understanding is particularly necessary for those entering the ministry of an established church. Being an evangelical (or, for that matter, an Anglo-Catholic or charismatic) Anglican incumbent entails a contradiction. On the one hand, there must be a commitment to all those living in the geographical parish. On the other hand, there is a commitment to a particular theology which may, in urban contexts, attract members to the congregation from way outside the parish. It is only when students explore the *sociological* dynamics of churches committed to the parish as against those committed to a particular theology that they realize how contradictory these commitments are (Reed, 1978). Evangelicals have an elective affinity with the sect form of organization, yet evangelical Anglicans find themselves within a long-established church. There is a contradiction between their theology and the sociological form of organization to which they have committed themselves.

In this contradiction lies the making or the breaking of the Anglican incumbent. One danger is to neglect the parish in favour of running a club for theologically pure commuters, causing untold hurt to local people who simply have nowhere else to go; another is to succumb uncritically to the folk religious demands of the parish. But the potential gains of parish ministry within the established church are enormous. Evangelical ministers committed to the parish, unlike their nonconformist counterparts in churches not organized on a parish system, cannot simply minister to those who agree with their theology, for they have to encounter the very real concerns of all those who live locally. The average vicar's workload around the death, funeral and bereavement of those who never come to church is a case in point (Walter, 1990). At its best, this earths evangelical theology in the real world, sharpening its understanding of the gospel. Hence the verdict with which this chapter began: 'It's only now that I at last understand why I'm going into the Anglican ministry.' Sociology can help evangelical students understand why they are going into the Anglican rather than, say, a Baptist ministry which on the surface looks more compatible with their theological stance.

What should be taught?

The two reasons I have given for including sociology of religion in theological training indicate two elements to the syllabus. The first is 'modernity and religion'; the second is 'church life and organization'.

First, the concept of modernity and what this means for religion (Hunter, 1994) is crucial. Modernity as an intellectual formation may not be a new idea to some evangelicals and charismatics, since criticisms of 'the Enlightenment' and of 'secular humanism' (Schaeffer, 1968) have been staple fare for conservative Christians for nearly thirty years now. Criticisms of the intellectual superstructure of modernity make little impact, however, so long as the sociological infrastructure of industrialization, urbanization, rationalization and pluralism remains unexamined.

Students need to consider how religion has changed in the modern world. Berger (1969) has argued that the pluralism and fragmentation of modern experience has reduced religion to a private experience, a personally chosen belief with little impact on society as a whole. The evangelical emphasis on personal decision and the charismatic emphasis on personal experience may or may not involve a recovery of New Testament Christianity, but they are certainly a response to modernity, locating Christianity within the private sphere and identifying it as a voluntary association, thereby leaving intact the secularism and pluralism of society as a whole. Only Islam seriously challenges this location for faith. Meanwhile charismatics continue to proclaim their God as Lord of all, while structurally this God has actually been reduced to a personal experience and a consumer choice.

At this point, Weber's (1976) Protestant ethic thesis demonstrates the sociologist's penchant for paradox and unexpected consequences: Protestant Christianity may well be implicated in the generation of the modern industrial society that has undermined the traditional power of religion.

All this inevitably stimulates students who hitherto had been asking themselves 'How can Christians affect society?' What sociology suggests is that Christians already have done, with paradoxical consequences, and that society has already affected Christians' understanding of their faith. The theological question thus becomes 'How are we to respond to the faith-society relationship that already exists?'

The question whether modernity is changing into something so radically different that it may be termed postmodern may be introduced at this point, along with whether the New Age, and possibly also the charismatic movement, might be understood as more recent responses to postmodernity. The vigorous debate on this issue (Bruce, 1996; Walker, 1997) not only induces students to think hard about present trends within the church, but also provides a sociological introduction to postmodernism, a concept that they encounter in more theological and philosophical parts of their degree.

Any sociological analysis of society raises the question of whether Christians should adapt to it, retreat from it or attempt to transform it (Niebuhr, H. R., 1929; Niebuhr, R., 1951). These theological questions can only be addressed seriously once students have begun to glimpse the depth and subtlety of the influence of culture, rather than seeing them as abstract questions to which various theologians have come to various conclusions.

Second, it seems to me that two ideas are particularly important to get across concerning church life and organiza-tion. One is that, whatever else it is, worship is a social and psychological phenomenon, and understanding this can greatly enhance the management of worship. This is readily grasped by looking at rites of passage (especially funerals), which both occupy much of the clergy's time and have been the subject of anthropological theorizing (Hertz, 1960; van Gennep, 1960). Covering this area is valuable in its own right, because it provides a perspective on the funerals that typically are otherwise somewhat neglected in theological training. More-over, through a consideration of Victor Turner's (1974) work, the perspective can be expanded from looking at occasional rites of passage to looking at Sunday worship. That there is a social/psychological framework to normal Sunday worship (as well as in 'emotionally manipulated' crusade meetings) can come as a revelation to some students. Reed's (1978) analysis of the dependency of congregations is particularly provocative, raising the question for those who are committed to participatory worship whether the leader should work with this dependency or challenge it (Walter, 1988).

A second key idea is that, whatever else they are, churches are organizations and function as such. The church–sect–denomination typology is a useful way to introduce the idea that organizational form can never in the long run be static. The way is then open to look at the question mentioned earlier: how does the evangelical or charismatic Christian operate within the structures of an established church? And a further question can now be re-asked: is the charismatic movement better understood not so much as a response to modernity/postmodernity, but rather as a response to the ossification of mainline churches? If the latter, does renewal *within* mainline denominations break the classic pattern of sect formation and is it likely to be more enduring than new breakaway churches? If all sects change in second and third generations, does this mean it is unwise to form breakaway churches?

Clearly many other issues concerning church life and organization can be examined, for example the clergy as a profession, or the role of gender within churches.

How should it be taught?

One can easily imagine, given the possibility of a sociology that 'explains away' religion, that one could have some very defensive students. In fact the very opposite can be the case. In this section, I describe the learning process as I have witnessed it.

First, the teacher presents a particular sociological theory as plausibly as possible, using examples with which the students can identify. It is important, therefore, that the teacher has experience of the society and of the churches which the students inhabit. Whether this experience has been gathered as a believer, or as a sociologist who has conducted research on such churches, is irrelevant. What matters is that students can see that the teacher has inside knowledge of their ecclesial world and respects that world. In my case, my view of churches in Britain has been very much a view from the pew (which, of course, coincides with the students' own experience to date); this is not true of all their lecturers, many of whom are ordained and whose view is more from pulpit, chancel and vicarage.

Second, students begin to see that the theory makes sense of their experience, perhaps more sense than that made hitherto by their repertoire of non-sociological and largely Christian concepts. It is not unusual for students to have 'Eureka!' insights. They are being seduced into accepting the theory.

Third, shock! At various points, students begin to wonder whether the theory *excludes* the supernatural, or at any rate challenges rather than complements their previous under-standings. But because the theory has been presented plausibly, they cannot instantly dismiss it. At this point, there is real engagement, the very stuff of teaching. Students are both wooed by the ability of the theory to explain many things better than do purely spiritual concepts, and disturbed by it.

Some students may fear that functionalist theories of religion explain it away. Others will point out that it is hardly surprising that obedience to divine law and acceptance of divine truth will lead to both social and individual well-being: it would be an odd kind of God who laid down rules that produce adverse consequences for societies that follow them! In other words, sociology can complement rather than undermine or bypass the student's faith. The pedagogical method here is to woo, seduce and disturb, so that the students have a real interest in working through these issues.

Fourth, by this time the teacher will have raised some of the standard criticisms of the theory in question. But whereas 20-year-old sociology students in a secular university would dutifully write down the criticisms, older theological students are passionately involved. Whether the theory in question is intellectually sound or not could have major implications for their future ministry.

To be resisted is the teaching style fashionable both in some conservative Christian circles and in A-level sociology, namely when introducing theories to label them as secular, humanist, Catholic, existential, feminist, Marxist, functionalist or whatever, thus enabling students not to take them seriously. The student is warned off the theory in advance and so stands no chance of the intellectual seduction that is so crucial to the pedagogy I am advocating. One student wrote in an end of term evaluation 'I have seen that it is quite unacceptable to attach a label, like "atheist" or "humanist" to a man's work, and then dismiss all that he has to say as a consequence.'

Fifth, in so far as students feel the theory does have some weight, there is then the question regarding how they should respond to it theologically and in future ministry. This question is inevitably raised by the students themselves.

Some students see such issues as affecting specific parts of their future ministry, such as funerals, evangelism, or whether charismatics should stay within or leave their denominations. For others, the very basis of their faith can be challenged. One London Bible College student told me that first-year teaching on biblical criticism had shattered his conviction that his faith was rooted in the objective truth of the written Word of God, so he did a lot of thinking and concluded that his faith had a surer foundation in his personal experience of the Holy Spirit. And then in his second year, wham, he encountered psychological theories of religion which provided convincing non-spiritual explanations for his spiritual experience. What was he left with? He did not lose his faith but continued searching, thinking and talking with faculty and fellow students.

This raises one crucial factor which determines whether encountering sociology and psychology of religion is a challenging and creative, or a disorienting and destructive, experience. The students whom I taught were studying within largely residential colleges that were, and are, deeply supportive of their students at many levels. Though committed to a clear theological stance, each college was also committed to facing reality rather than running away from it, and this was reflected within the student subculture.

A final factor that can influence whether the students' experience of the sociology of religion is constructive is that the teacher, if not a believer him or herself, should at the very least respect the students' beliefs and commitment to ministry. Throughout, my style was not to debunk their world but to illuminate it. When constructively challenged by sociological

Tony Walter

perspectives, students find the teacher a friend with whom they
can thrash things out, not an adversary to be knocked down –
or prayed for!

References

Berger, P. (1969), *The Social Reality of Religion*, London, Faber &
Faber.
Bruce, S. (1996), *Religion in the Modern World: From Cathedrals to
Cults*, Oxford, Oxford University Press.
Hertz, R. (1960), *Death and the Right Hand*, London, Cohen & West.
Hunter, J. D. (1994), What is modernity? in P. Sampson, V. Samuel
and C. Sugden (eds), *Faith and Modernity*, pp. 12–28, Oxford,
Regnum.
Newbigin, L. (1989), *The Gospel in a Pluralist Society*, London,
SPCK.
Niebuhr, H. R. (1929), *The Social Sources of Denominationalism*,
New York, Holt.
Niebuhr, R. (1951), *Christ and Culture*, New York, Harper.
Reed, B. (1978), *The Dynamics of Religion*, London, Darton,
Longman & Todd.
Schaeffer, F. (1968), *Escape from Reason*, London, IVP.
Turner, V. (1974), *The Ritual Process*, Harmondsworth, Penguin.
van Gennep, A. (1960), *The Rites of Passage*, Chicago, University of
Chicago Press.
Walker, A. (1997), Thoroughly modern: reflections on the charis-
matic movement, in S. Hunt, M. Hamilton and T. Walter (eds),
Charismatic Christianity: Sociological Perspectives, pp. 17–42,
Basingstoke, Macmillan.
Walter, T. (1988), Against participation, for the Kingdom, *Church-
man*, 102, 143–50.
Walter, T. (1990), *Funerals: And How to Improve Them*, London,
Hodder.
Weber, M. (1976), *The Protestant Ethic and the Spirit of Capitalism*,
London, Unwin.

8

Is Self-assigned Religious Affiliation Socially Significant?

Rosalind S. Fane

Introduction

T his question is given point by the debate over whether citizens in England, Scotland and Wales should be asked to state their religious affiliations (assign themselves a religious label) in the national Census of Population. The debate itself arises from a disjunction between the conviction of Britain's faith communities that religion should be taken seriously by the government, and the government's need to be convinced that religion is socially relevant. Cross-cultural comparisons reveal this type of tension even in countries where it has long been common practice for the population census routinely to include a question on religious affiliation. This chapter argues that the tension persists primarily because our understanding of this variable is underdeveloped at both a conceptual and an empirical level. Conceptually, there is a tendency either to conflate religious affiliation with markers of religiosity measuring practice or belief, or to assume it to be an inaccurate indicator of practice and belief. Empirically, the relative significance of religious affiliation, in its own right, as a predictor of social attitudes and behaviours has not been adequately established or acknowledged.

Rosalind S. Fane

Identifying the social face of religion

The concept of religion is notoriously difficult to define, even harder to operationalize for the purposes of empirical analysis. The introduction has referred to religion in terms of affiliation, practice and belief. There are, of course, many more possible dimensions that could be discerned. Grichting (1985, p. 4) reports that attempts to theorize the components of religion have resulted in the identification of between one and eleven dimensions. Smart (1992), a prime exemplar of multi-dimensional analyses of religion, conceptualizes a religion as comprising seven elements: the experiential, the ritual, the mythic, the doctrinal, the ethical, the social and the material. Black and Glasner (1983, p. 183), referring to Smart's (1971) six-dimensional model of religion (Smart's seven dimensions minus the material aspect) loosely describe the doctrinal, mythological and ethical dimensions as *beliefs*, and the ritual, experiential and social dimensions as *practices*.

This juxtaposition of 'inward convictions' and 'outward practices' (Sharpe, 1983, p. 37), or the private and the public, is a common analytical device in the social scientific study of religion. Davie's (1994, p. 76) characterization of religion in modern Britain in terms of 'believing without belonging' was intended to sum up a situation in which religious belief has become 'privatized'; in other words widely held in the individual psyche but no longer publicly affirmed through church attendance. Francis and Mullen (1993, 1995) have also emphasized the importance of distinguishing between the implicit (personal belief) and the explicit (public worship) elements which constitute an individual's religiosity.

This dichotomy does not, however, provide adequate scope for the theorization of religious affiliation as an indicator of the social influence of religion. The frequent use of religious affiliation as a measure of religion in population censuses worldwide seems to be governed less by a theoretically and empirically informed rationale than by a sense of what it is deemed acceptable to ask the general public (see, for example, Statistics New Zealand, 1998, p. 112). In the context of a population census, the sociological distinction between private (belief) and public (practice) is inadequate. The public practice of religion actually becomes an extremely private matter, which seems rarely to be made the focus of a census question. Consequently, there is confusion over what information on the population's religious affiliations actually means and how it might be used.

Evidence from New Zealand, where a question on religious affiliation is routinely asked in the national population census, confirms this to be a serious problem. A recent information paper produced in preparation for the 2001 Census of Population and Dwellings in New Zealand stated that '[T]he practical value of census information on religion is questionable, particularly in view of the fact that it does not provide an accurate indication of either the church-going practices of the population or the depth of a person's commitment to their specified religion' (Statistics New Zealand, 1998, p. 112). Three assumptions lie behind this statement: first, religious affiliation does not predict church attendance and depth of commitment with sufficient accuracy to make it a useful empirical variable; second, religious affiliation is not socially significant in its own right; and third, church attendance and depth of commitment (however this is measured) are likely to be better indicators of the social influence of religion than religious affiliation.

The problem of nominalism

The first assumption arises from the problem of nominalism. In the 1991 Canadian Census, over 80 per cent of the population claimed to belong to a Christian group, although less than a third of Canadians regularly attend church (O'Toole, 1996, p. 122). With reference to the 1981 New Zealand Census, Hill and Bowman (1985, p. 92) note that approximately 75 per cent of the population adopted a religious label, but estimate the corresponding number of regular church attenders to be as few as 10 per cent of the population. A self-assigned religious label then may, but disproportionately may not, indicate regular church attendance.

However, when the focus of religious affiliation is sharpened by denominational identity, it becomes potentially much more useful as a predictor of church attendance. For example, based on findings from the 1991 National Church Life Survey, Hughes (1997, pp. 8, 10, 40) reports that while only 4.8 per cent of self-identified Anglicans attend church in a typical week, the corresponding figure for Lutherans is 20 per cent, and for Baptists as many as 37 per cent. Similarly, distinct relationships between denominational identity and patterns of church attendance, prayer, self-perceived religiousness, importance of God in life and the nature of belief in God were found by Bouma and Dixon (1986) in another Australian study. Right-wing Protestants, mainline Protestants, Anglicans, Catholics and 'nones' were all confirmed as distinct groups in terms of type and level of religiosity.

The assumption, then, that religious affiliation cannot be used as a proxy for other markers of religious commitment is not entirely accurate. This section has suggested that it *may* be useful, particularly where information on denominational identity is also available. Even so, is this really the most effective way in which such data could be used to measure religion's social significance? The highly complex interrelationship between religious affiliation, practice and belief in the make-up of an individual's religiosity is well illustrated by Francis and Mullen's (1993, p. 667) 'multi-level classification': unaffiliated atheists (non-attender, non-believer), affiliated atheists (non-attender, non-believer), unaffiliated agnostics (non-attender, believer or non-believer), affiliated agnostics (non-attender, believer or non-believer), unaffiliated believers (non-attender, believer), affiliated believers (non-attender, believer), believers attending occasionally (affiliated or unaffiliated), believers attending regularly (affiliated or unaffiliated).

Given that it is impossible to distinguish between the numerous religiosity types that can potentially be represented on a census through the claiming of a religious label, the futility of attempting to look behind the label in this way is self-evident. This is especially true in the context of high levels of Christian nominalism, where information on denominational identity is not available, as would be the case in the census of England, Scotland and Wales. Unlike in Australia, Canada and New Zealand, there is no plan to subdivide the Christian category were a question on religion to be asked (Office for National Statistics, 1998, p. 8).

Is self-assigned religious affiliation socially significant?

This chapter now goes on to challenge the second assumption, outlined above, that religious affiliation, in its own right, is not an indicator of the social significance of religion by asking, does a self-assigned religious label significantly determine certain social attitudes and behaviours? There is a growing body of empirical research into the relative predictive power of religion, analysed along its various dimensions. In some cases, researchers have begun to consider the implications of the findings for public policy. Such research is conducted in relation to a wide range of social issues including: substance use (see for a review, Gorsuch, 1995); health and well-being (see for reviews, Koenig, 1997; Matthews, McCullough, Larson, Koenig, Swyers and Milano, 1998); and general values (see for example, Bouma and Dixon, 1986; Webster and Perry, 1989; Hoffmann and Miller, 1997). Although the level of complexity of this type of research varies, religious affiliation, practice and belief (the dimensions of religion on which this chapter focuses) have all been found to correlate, to varying degrees depending on the issue, with attitudes and behaviours. For example, research into adolescent attitudes to substance use variously found: frequency of church attendance and different Christian denominational identities significantly predicts attitudes towards alcohol (Francis, 1992, p. 49); there is a correlation between drinking behaviour and denominational identity, but not between drinking behaviour and frequency of church attendance (Francis, 1994, p. 31); denominational identity and belief are better predictors of attitudes towards heroin than church attendance, but church attendance is a better predictor of attitudes towards alcohol than denominational identity and belief (Francis and Mullen, 1993, p. 670); and denominational identity significantly influences attitudes towards drug use, but only when this identity is supported by church attendance (Francis and Mullen, 1997, p. 91).

There is evidence, then, to suggest that religious affiliation is, in its own right, socially significant, particularly when it is subdivided by denomination. Moreover, to refute the third assumption, outlined above, religious affiliation is not necessarily a less significant predictor than religious practice and belief. In light of this and drawing on the work of Bouma

(1992), it is now suggested that, in terms of interpreting census data, it may be helpful to conceptualize religious affiliation more as a key component of social identity, and less as an inadequate proxy for religious practice and belief.

Towards an alternative conceptualization of religious affiliation

Bouma's (1992) sociological theory of religious identification (he does not use the word affiliation) can be divided into two main parts. First, he analyses religious identity (a self-assigned religious label) in terms of its *distinction* from religious belief, church attendance and other common markers of church-orientated religiosity. Thus, Bouma is not concerned with what religious identification might indicate in terms of orthodox religious commitment. This marks a clear departure from the problematic approach outlined previously in the chapter. Instead, Bouma (1992, p. 110) defines religious identification as a 'useful social category giving some indication of the cultural background and general orientating values of a person'. Second, he posits a process through which 'cultural background' and 'general orientating values' are acquired. Importantly, this process of acquisition is exactly the same for religious identity as it is for political or sporting or philosophical identities, and consists of: first, 'meaning systems', which Bouma (1992, p. 106) describes as '... a set or collection of answers to questions about the meaning and purpose of life'; and second, 'plausibility structures' (borrowed from Berger 1967, 1969), which Bouma (1992, p. 107) describes as 'social arrangements which serve to inculcate, celebrate, perpetuate and apply a meaning system'. He maintains that all of us possess meaning systems from which we derive our existential purpose. He cites a living church as being one example of a plausibility structure through which a meaning system is, literally, made plausible and then disseminated. Although a self-assigned religious identity might also imply commitment to a plausibility structure (practice) and adherence to its related meaning system (belief), Bouma (1992, p. 108) suggests that it might be equally, perhaps more, significant in terms of the exposure to the particular cultural background that it represents. Crucially, this alternative conceptualization avoids the difficult terrain of religious affiliation as proxy for practice and belief by recognizing that even non-church attenders and non-believers 'may still show *the effect* of the meaning system and plausibility structure with which they identify' (Bouma, 1992, p. 108, my emphasis).

The value of Bouma's sociological theory of religious identification is that it allows us to perceive, and thus analyse, a self-assigned religious affiliation as a key component of social identity, in a way similar to age, gender, class location, political persuasion, nationality, ethnic group and others (see Zavalloni, 1975, p. 200). It informs our attitudes and, in turn, our modes of behaviour by contributing to our self-definition both of who we are, but equally importantly, of who we are not. This type of analysis is especially advantageous when interpreting census data, because it is inclusive of all those who claim a religious affiliation, not only of the minority who also attend church. Referring back to the inadequacy of the sociological distinction between belief and practice for understanding the significance of affiliation, it is, to some extent, overcome by the concept of identity which, in Beit-Hallahmi's (1991, p. 91) words 'seems to provide a bridge between the private and the public realms in religion as an appropriate locus for that which connects the individual personality and the cultural matrix'.

To pre-empt the criticism that to conceptualize religious affiliation as a component of social identity is to run the risk of negating the importance of theology altogether, the final section now turns to a consideration of the source of the social significance of self-assigned religious affiliation. In the context of a nominal Christian majority and drawing on the work of Bibby (1985, 1987), it argues that the mainspring of a religious label's social significance may actually (still) be located within the orthodox/traditional tenets of the faith to which it refers.

The problem of nominalism revisited

Bibby (1985) has sought to explain a situation characterized by a high number of Christian affiliates but a correspondingly low number of regular church attenders, by positing a theory of 'religious encasement'. Following up 1980–81 national survey data, which found nearly nine out of ten Canadians claimed a Protestant or Roman Catholic label, while only one in three regularly attended church, Bibby asked Canadians to 'assess the nature of their religion'. He found that 85 per cent of affiliated Protestants and Roman Catholics described themselves as religious to some degree. Furthermore, amongst the 15 per cent who claimed not to be religious, two-thirds reported some, albeit occasional, contact with a church. These findings, combined with those from an earlier national survey high-lighting the continuity of Christian affiliation, between and within generations, and its prominence as a chosen identity for those whose parents have no religious affiliation, form the basis for Bibby's argument that Canadian Christians are 'encased' within the Christian tradition. In other words, this tradition has a strong, influential hold over both its active and latent members from which affiliates find it extremely difficult to extricate themselves.

Bibby then identifies four types of religious commitment displayed by Christian affiliates who are, by his definition, encased within the Christian tradition. Those who describe themselves as 'committed Christians' are equally divided between the traditionally committed (believing in God, the divinity of Jesus and life after death; praying privately; experiencing God; and having some knowledge of the Bible) and the non-traditionally committed (who display these characteristics inconsistently). For both groups, Bibby (1985, p. 299) maintains, 'Christianity functions as a fairly compre-hensive meaning system.' For those Christians who describe themselves as less committed, Christianity does not, according to Bibby, provide an overarching meaning system in their lives. Instead they are free-riders who draw on it selectively, particularly at the time of a birth, marriage or death. Finally, the individuals comprising the 15 per cent who, in the earlier part of Bibby's survey described themselves as 'non-religious', exhibit a 'fragmented' commitment to traditional Christian tenets. As many as 30 per cent of these engaged in personal private prayer and professed a belief in God, but hardly any attended church.

However, Bibby (1985, p. 300) is keen to emphasize the permeability of these categories: 'The proportion of affiliates exhibiting each of these four dominant kinds of commitment is ever-changing within the religious casings, analogous to mercury floating in glass tubing.' The type of commitment that Christian affiliates exhibit at any one time varies between and within denominations. Contrary to the claims of secularization theorists that low levels of church attendance are indicative of the erosion of religion's social significance (see Wallis and Bruce, 1992), Bibby (1985, 1987) would argue that this trend is actually a manifestation of the repackaging of religion in the context of late twentieth-century consumer-oriented society. Consumers, as we all are, are free to select 'fragments' of faith, and we are encouraged to do this by the way in which the churches have simulated the marketing strategies of the wider society.

The central point to glean from Bibby's analysis is that the potential for religion, in this case Christianity, to be a socially significant attitudinal and behavioural determinant has not necessarily disappeared. If anything, the Christian 'casing' may have been strengthened, because the accommodationist stance adopted by the Christian churches has, according to Bibby, reduced the need for affiliates to look elsewhere. In sum, Bibby (1985, p. 300) explains the paradox of high levels of religious affiliation but correspondingly low levels of church attendance, characteristic of contemporary Christianity in Canada, not by projecting the demise of religion but by arguing that Christian affiliates are tending to choose 'uncommitment over commitment, and fragments over meaning systems'. The fact remains, however, that all four groups of Christian affiliates identified by Bibby, from the 'traditionally committed' to the 'non-religious' are, to a greater or lesser extent, influenced by beliefs and practices central to the Christian faith. It may still be worth looking here when trying to locate the source of the social significance of self-assigned religious, in this case Christian, affiliation.

These assertions resonate with Davie's (1994, p. 76) analysis of the continuing salience of the religious roots of Christianity in modern Britain. She too is keen to emphasize the origin of the beliefs which shape the nominal Christian community in modern Britain and urges the use of the term 'common', in preference to the term 'privatized', to describe Christian nominalism lest the origins of this 'religion' be overlooked. To elaborate, she argues that '[T]here is, in fact, no real gap between orthodox theologies and wider patterns of believing. The relationship between the two is a complex one, but it is better described as a continuum than as a dichotomy, in that very few individuals escape the influence of common religion altogether.'

Conclusion

Self-assigned religious affiliation may be useful as a predictor of other markers of religiosity such as practice and belief, particularly when sub-divided by denomination, but self-assigned religious affiliation may also be useful as a predictor of social attitudes and behaviours, particularly when sub-divided by denomination. In relation to other markers of religiosity such as practice and belief, self-assigned religious affiliation, as a potential social predictor, should be seen as differently significant, rather than less significant.

In analyses of census data, it may prove helpful to conceptualize self-assigned religious affiliation as a component of social identity, rather than as an inadequate indicator of religious practice and belief. The advantage of this strategy is that it widens the scope of religious affiliation as an empirical variable, by allowing for shifts in forms of religious commitment. This is not to deny the importance of orthodox theological tenets. On the contrary, it is to suggest they may still be socially significant in the lives of *all* affiliates.

References

Beit-Hallahmi, B. (1991), Religion and identity: concepts, data, questions, *Social Science Information*, 30, 81–95.
Berger, P. (1967), *The Sacred Canopy: Elements of a Sociology of Religion*, New York, Doubleday.
Berger, P. (1969), *A Rumor of Angels: Modern Society and the Rediscovery of the Supernatural*, New York, Doubleday.
Bibby, R. W. (1985), Religious encasement in Canada: an argument for Protestant and Catholic entrenchment, *Social Compass*, 16, 287–303.
Bibby, R. W. (1987), *Fragmented Gods: The Poverty and Potential of Religion in Canada*, Toronto, Irwin Publishing.
Black, A. and Glasner, P. (eds) (1983), Conclusion, in A. Black and P. Glasner (eds), *Practice and Belief*, pp. 181–6, Sydney, George Allen and Unwin.
Bouma, G. D. (1992), *Religion: Meaning, Transcendence and*

Community in Australia, Melbourne, Longman Cheshire.

Bouma, G. D. and Dixon, B. R. (1986), *The Religious Factor in Australian Life*, Melbourne, MARC Australia.

Davie, G. (1994), *Religion in Modern Britain since 1945*, Oxford, Blackwell.

Francis, L. J. (1992), Attitude towards alcohol, church attendance and denominational identity, *Drug and Alcohol Dependence*, 31, 45–50.

Francis, L. J. (1994), Denominational identity, church attendance and drinking behaviour among adults in England, *Journal of Alcohol and Drug Education*, 39, 27–33.

Francis, L. J. and Mullen, K. (1993), Religiosity and attitudes towards drug use among 13–15 year olds in England, *Addiction*, 88, 665–72.

Francis, L. J. and Mullen, K. (1995), Religiosity and attitudes towards drug use among Dutch school children, *Journal of Alcohol and Drug Education*, 41, 16–25.

Francis, L. J. and Mullen, K. (1997), Denominational and sectarian influence on adolescent attitude towards drug use in England and Wales, *Journal of Alcohol and Drug Education*, 42, 81–96.

Gorsuch, R. L. (1995), Religious aspects of substance abuse and recovery, *Journal of Social Issues*, 51, 65–83.

Grichting, W. L. (1985), *Dimensions of Religiosity: Degree, Domain and Context*, unpublished manuscript, Department of Behavioural Sciences, James Cook University of North Queensland.

Hill, M. and Bowman, R. (1985), Religious adherence and religious practice in contemporary New Zealand: census and survey evidence, *Archives de Sciences Sociales des Religions*, 59, 91–112.

Hoffmann, J. P. and Miller, A. S. (1997), Social and political attitudes among religious groups: convergence and divergence over time, *Journal for the Scientific Study of Religion*, 36, 52–70.

Hughes, P. J. (1997), *Religion in Australia: Facts and Figures*, Kew, Victoria, Christian Research Association.

Koenig, H. G. (1997), *Is Religion Good for Your Health? The Effects of Religion on Physical and Mental Health*, New York, Haworth Pastoral Press.

Matthews, D. A., McCullough, M. E., Larson, D. B., Koenig, H. G., Swyers, J. P. and Milano, M. G. (1998), Religious commitment and health status: a review of the research and implications for family medicine, *Archives of Family Medicine*, 7, 118–24.

Office for National Statistics (1998), *1998 Census Test: Cognitive Testing of the Religion Question*, unpublished manuscript.

O'Toole, R. (1996), Religion in Canada: its development and contemporary situation, *Social Compass*, 43, 119–34.

Sharpe, E. J. (1983), *Understanding Religion*, London, Gerald Duckworth.

Smart, N. (1971), *The Religious Experience of Mankind*, London, Fontana.

Smart, N. (1992), *The World's Religions*, Cambridge, Cambridge University Press.

Statistics New Zealand (1998), *2001 Census of Population and Dwellings: Preliminary Views on Content*, Wellington, Publishing and Media Services Division of Statistics New Zealand.

Wallis, R. and Bruce, S. (1992), Secularization: the orthodox model, in S. Bruce (ed.), *Religion and Modernization: Sociologists and Historians Debate the Secularization Thesis*, pp. 8–30, Oxford, Clarendon Press.

Webster, A. C. and Perry, P. E. (1989), *The Religious Factor in New Zealand Society*, Palmerston North, Alpha Publications.

Zavalloni, M. (1975), Social identity and the Recording of Reality: Its Relevance for Cross-cultural Psychology, *International Journal of Psychology*, 10, 197–217.

Part III   Empirical Perspectives

9

The Socialization of Glossolalia

Mark J. Cartledge

Introduction

T he charismatic movement is now very influential globally.
  Yet it is only recently that studies have been undertaken
which combine different approaches to it such as sociology and
theology together. The focus of the present study is the
phenomenon of speaking in tongues, otherwise known as
glossolalia (Malony and Lovekin, 1985; Poloma, 1989). For
charismatics, the gift of tongues is understood to be a language
of worship and prayer, and as such a means of communication
with God. Classical Pentecostals understood glossolalia to be
the definitive sign of an overwhelming experience of the Holy
Spirit called baptism in the Spirit. Initially those involved in
traditional denominations also understood it in this way.
However, with the influence of the Third Wave Movement,
focused around the ministry of John Wimber and the Vineyard
denomination, this specific emphasis has waned. The New
Church Movement, formerly called the House Church Movement, combines a variety of Pentecostal and charismatic
strands together, but it also seeks to develop its own unique
approach (Walker, 1985; Scotland, 1994). The church in this
study is to be located within this New Church Movement.

For research purposes, I use the working definition of
charismatic glossolalia proposed by Poythress (1980) who sees
glossolalia as a form of free vocalization:

Free vocalization (glossolalia) occurs when (1) a
human being produces a connected sequence of
speech sounds, (2) he cannot identify the sound-
sequence as belonging to any natural language that
he already knows how to speak, (3) he cannot
identify and give the meaning of words or mor-
phemes (minimal lexical units), (4) in the case of
utterances of more than a few syllables, he typically
cannot repeat the same sound-sequence on demand,
(5) a naïve listener might suppose that it was an
unknown language.

Poythress uses the term T-speech (tongues) to refer to Christian
free vocalization within the context of worship.

This essay reviews case-study materials concerning the
theological praxis (belief and practice) of glossolalia which
suggest that glossolalia is acquired by means of socialization.
By socialization is meant the process by which a person learns
the meanings of a culture or subculture, identifies with them
and is shaped by them. As Peter Berger (1973, p. 25) says, 'He
draws them into himself and makes them his meanings. He
becomes not only one who possesses these meanings, but one
who represents and expresses them.' The most important
discussion of this idea in relation to glossolalia is by William J.
Samarin (1969, 1972, 1973) who combines his insights as both a
linguist and anthropologist, in sociolinguistic terms, to argue
that glossolalia is more properly understood as a learned
experience. In other words, the social context, at the very least,
provides certain clues which enable the individual to take a
'jump into the dark' and speak in tongues (Samarin, 1972, p.
55).

Samarin's data include responses to a questionnaire and a
transcription of a tape-recording of a Full Gospel Business
Men's Fellowship meeting where people were invited to receive
the baptism in the Spirit. There were 84 questionnaire
responses from different groups in Canada, Germany, England,
Holland and the United States. They were mostly from middle-
class Protestant members of the charismatic movement rather
than established Pentecostal groups. Samarin investigated the
acquisition of glossolalia by means of questions concerning: the
desire to speak in tongues, friends and family who spoke in

tongues, encouragement or exhortation, instruction or guidance about what might occur, difficulties encountered, first
experience and expectations and the improvement of one's
ability to speak in tongues as time passed.

Samarin argues that glossolalia cannot be learned in the
sense that one would learn a normal human language. This is
because each tongue speech is produced more or less *de novo*.
However, in another sense, glossolalia is learned because it is
associated with becoming a member of a social group. The
main requirement for someone to speak in tongues is a desire to
do so as part of a search for a new or better religious
experience. Often the instruction concerning tongues given to
those seeking baptism in the Spirit is minimal. It may contain
some instruction to submit oneself to God and to relax. This
can be supplemented in a number of ways. For instance, a
person may be advised: to speak whatever comes to mind; or to
'make sounds' of any kind, with allusions often made to
childlike speech; or to imitate the utterances of others as they
speak in tongues; or to repeat a brief meaningless utterance
(which has already come to mind) in the hope that fluent
productive glossolalia will follow; or to repeat a meaningful
word or phrase, like 'El Shaddai' or 'Praise Jesus' as a means of
speaking in tongues. Such instruction is often accompanied by
an expectant atmosphere, constructed by the use of silence,
hushed voices, the rhetoric of the preacher and the 'laying on of
hands' (Samarin, 1972, pp. 50–58). However, Samarin qualifies
these comments by saying that the social setting in which the
acquisition of glossolalia occurs appears to be so varied as to
make it irrelevant (Samarin, 1972, p. 61). But the question is
whether there is some underlying social influence which
transcends local variations.

According to Samarin, the language-learning instruction is to
be summarized by saying that the respondents to his
questionnaire were given no clear model as to how to speak
in tongues, and that many of them had not heard glossolalia for
long enough to conceive their own model of it. They knew
neither the phonological elements required to produce glossolalia nor how to group these elements together in speech. All
that they understood was that whatever they said would be
'real words from a real language unknown to themselves'
(Samarin, 1969, p. 62). In addition, Samarin argues that there

will always be a few people for whom this minimal instruction does not apply. These people find themselves speaking in tongues without intending to do so, privately and without any knowledge of the Pentecostal and charismatic traditions.

For Samarin the instruction which is given in meetings is of little linguistic importance. Someone who has been exposed to glossolalia, however, can retain enough information so that he or she is able to use the same sound, intonation and paralinguistic devices. He suggests that it is more likely that glossolalic patterns be passed on within the circle of those who already speak in tongues. Therefore, glossolalic control improves and people learn to use it in different ways (Samarin, 1973, p. 87).

In summary, Samarin argues that the desire for deeper spiritual experience, when linked to the influences of people and information located in the various contexts, predispose individuals to speak in tongues. The implicit assumptions within the charismatic movement create contexts in which the seeker is able to take a 'jump into the dark' and begin speaking in tongues.

The aim of this study is to explore Samarin's thesis in relation to material collected from a case study of an Independent Charismatic Church in Liverpool. All names mentioned in this account are pseudonyms.

Method

The case-study method (Yin, 1984, 1993; Stake, 1995) was employed since this method enables an investigation within the real-life context when the boundaries between the phenomenon and the context are not clearly evident (Yin, 1984, p. 23). Within the overall case-study strategy other methods were used.

Participant observation was carried out over a period of seven months during which I visited Sunday worship on eight occasions (May, 1993; Silverman, 1993). Documents relating to the church life were analysed, including Sunday news-sheets, foundation documents written at the church's inception, the Alpha course material used by the church (Holy Trinity Church Brompton, 1993), and the book by Nicky Gumbel (1994). Semi-structured interviews were conducted on nine occasions with a total of thirteen people taking part. The interviews were tape recorded and subsequently transcribed (Berg, 1989; May, 1993; Silverman, 1993). Some of the interview questions targeted the relevant areas of church background and Christian experience, initial and current experience of glossolalia, frequency of use, contexts and sources of understanding or interpretation. Data analysis was conducted with the assistance of a free-form text retrieval system (Dey, 1993).

Results

All of those interviewed had wished to receive spiritual gifting from God when they initially found themselves speaking in tongues. Five specifically emphasized the fact that they had been seeking the gift (Steven, Rebecca, Ruth, Emily and Rachel), although the circumstances varied. For Steven in particular, the biblical injunction of 1 Corinthians 14:1, that one should 'eagerly desire spiritual gifts', was inspirational. However, all were influenced by some of the biblical teaching on the matter of spiritual gifts and glossolalia as it is mediated through the contemporary charismatic movement.

Most interviewees were able to confirm that they had been encouraged to speak in tongues by someone they knew or had met. Five specifically linked it to their experience of baptism in the Spirit (Steven, Kate, Robert, Philip and Adam), while one associated an initial experience of glossolalia with her water baptism (Rachel). Another person received the gift while seeking it privately at home (Rebecca). Three others received explicit instructions while seeking to speak in tongues.

First, Jane told the story of how she was prayed over by a Baptist minister friend and his wife. She was told to say whatever came to mind at a later time, when she was expected to pray at home. In other words, she was to verbalize what sounds came into mind. This she was able to do and remembers consciously deciding to say the 'words' which she had in her mind.

Second, Ruth had also been prayed for in order to receive the gift. The advice she received, after a failed attempt two years previously, was to be 'practical'. She should not expect tongues to suddenly flow, but she had to speak aloud any syllables which came to mind. This she was able to do. Subsequently, some time later, she attended a charismatic camp seminar on the subject of praying for a 'new' tongue. This she received and discovered it to be better than the 'old' one, to which she never returned.

Third, Emily had been seeking the gift for some time but to no avail. She had been helping at a children's camp where the children had been speaking in tongues. She was frustrated by her own inability and sought counsel. She was advised that there was nothing that anyone else could do, that she had to do it herself. She was disappointed at the time but later 'decided' to do it. She said one 'word' and kept repeating that 'word' over and over again. She felt that it was like a baby language one had to repeat and practise. Subsequently more 'words' were added until she became fluent.

All the informants, except Julie, had experienced other forms of charismatic Christianity before coming to the church which was the object of the study. In most cases it appeared that the wider charismatic scene has more influence than their present church. Here tongues are rarely used in public. Therefore the socialization of people into the acceptance of glossolalia occurs largely from previous church experience or wider charismatic contact.

Finally, most of the interviewees felt that they had developed their glossolalia through some form of practice. More 'words' came as existing 'words' were used. Thus the speech became more fluent as longer time periods were spent using it. More purpose was developed and different uses discovered (worship, intercession and spiritual warfare). Only two people felt that their glossolalia had declined in recent times. Philip felt that his use of tongues had declined through lack of practice, thus the habit had changed, while Adam believed speaking in tongues was now drier and less exciting than it had been previously. He preferred the use of silence when praying, but noticed that during a time of crisis he returned to using it. Finally, Basil had declared himself a non-tongues speaker. He had at one point received one 'word' in his mind but felt unable to proceed. He dismissed his inability to speak in tongues as due to being a linguist and a Latin teacher! He has nevertheless felt edified by the tongue speech of others.

Discussion

It is inevitable that the person's desire to speak in tongues is informed by the charismatic tradition which he or she has encountered. The gift of tongues is legitimized by reference to the Bible which informs the basic perceptions of reality (or world-view) through which the phenomenon is socialized. The variety of social contexts in which people learn and practise glossolalia indicates, as Samarin suggests, that the social setting is very varied and perhaps not as stereotyped as might be thought in terms of the acquisition of glossolalia. In the church under study the public use of tongues is infrequent and largely limited to singing in tongues. This means that informants utilize the leaders and literature of the wider charismatic movement to support and reinforce their belief and practice. This is confirmed by the fact that only one informant (Julie) encountered tongues initially at the church, where it was associated with becoming a Christian and joining a social group. Socialization occurred here but more significantly at the Good News Crusade Camp and other occasions where the social expectation to practise glossolalia was considerably higher. It is also clear that those whose practice of glossolalia had decreased were people who had less contact, and therefore less continued socialization, with the wider charismatic movement than others interviewed (Philip and Adam) (Berger, 1973, p. 26).

Although the social contexts vary immensely there appears to be a socialization process in operation. It may be expressed in weaker terms at one end of the spectrum, for example being 'encouraged' to speak in tongues, or by simply picking up the clues from the social context. Alternatively, it can be expressed in more explicit terms at the other end of the spectrum, where the instructions given to seekers are clearly expressed. Both extremes are located within the data from the case study. The development of tongue speech recorded in the data also coheres with what Samarin describes. People develop their ability to speak in tongues not in isolation but within a Christian community, within continued socialization. Therefore it is not surprising that individuals will consciously or unconsciously adopt certain language styles and perceptions which reflect their particular group, and in some cases other groups as well.

However, this socialization interpretation simply draws out the largely implicit (but sometimes explicit) influences at work throughout the charismatic movement. Further research is required to elucidate the nature of the glossolalic experience for the minority who do not fit into this category. That is, those people who suddenly find themselves speaking in tongues without having any charismatic socialization whatsoever.

In theological terms, the charismatic world-view is informed by the text of Scripture. The precise relationship between glossolalia in the New Testament and today is still a matter of debate (Turner, 1996). This study shows that any sociological interpretation of contemporary glossolalia cannot be considered in isolation from the theological material which informs and legitimates the contemporary belief and practice. On this matter theology and sociology must dialogue (and one would wish to invite to this discussion the other behavioural sciences also).

Conclusion

The approach which sees glossolalia as human behaviour and therefore as something which is influenced by the way people learn in general terms must be acknowledged. That glossolalia is a phenomenon which is always explicitly taught within the Pentecostal and charismatic movements is to be doubted. Rather it is something which grows within a charismatic plausibility structure that validates the belief and practice of it. From a theological perspective, the acknowledgement that glossolalia is mostly acquired and clearly developed through socialization does not necessarily nullify the notion that glossolalia is also a gift of the Holy Spirit. Theology cannot be reduced to sociology without serious loss of identity. Rather a combined approach affirms the idea that within the charismata grace works in and through human nature, including socialization processes. As Max Turner (1996, p. 310) argues,

> even a 'learned behaviour' or a form of utterance initially psychologically induced might (in God's grace, and when directed to him in a doxology of love) *become* a 'supernatural' divine gift (even if not

a 'miraculous' one), in the same fashion as a person's natural teaching gifts may become on occasion the spiritual gift of powerful preaching that 'brings all heaven down' to listeners.

Therefore theology and sociology may both illuminate the contemporary phenomenon of glossolalia in complementary terms. This sociological perspective also highlights the limitations of the socialization theory: it cannot explain or interpret glossolalia adequately (Hine, 1969, p. 221). Rather it identifies the importance of the wider sociological base in relation to which most, if not all, acquire and sustain glossolalia. It is in this sense that the perspective of Samarin can be understood to shed light on the social settings in which the prospective tongue speaker takes a 'jump into the dark'. It is theology which begins to illuminate that darkness, or mystery, and helps practitioners and critics alike understand something of the significance of charismatic glossolalic praxis (Baker, 1996).

References

Baker, H. G. (1996), *Pentecostal Experience: Towards a Reconstructive Theology of Glossolalia*, Unpublished PhD dissertation, King's College, University of London.

Berg, B. L. (1989), *Qualitative Research Methods for the Social Sciences*, Boston, Allyn and Bacon.

Berger, P. L. (1973), *The Social Reality of Religion*, Harmondsworth, Penguin.

Dey, I. (1993), *Qualitative Data Analysis*, London, Routledge.

Gumbel, N. (1994), *A Life Worth Living*, Eastbourne, Kingsway.

Hine, V. H. (1969), Pentecostal Glossolalia: Toward a Functional Interpretation, *Journal for the Scientific Study of Religion*, 8, 211–26.

Holy Trinity Church Brompton (1993), *Alpha Training Manual*, London, Holy Trinity Brompton Publication.

Malony, H. N. and Lovekin A. A. (1985), *Glossolalia: Behavioural Science Perspectives on Speaking in Tongues*, Oxford, Oxford University Press.

May, T. (1993), *Social Research Issues, Methods and Process*, Buckingham, Open University Press.

Poloma, M. M. (1989), *The Assemblies of God at the Crossroads: Charisma and Institutional Dilemmas*, Knoxville, University of Tennessee Press.

Mark J. Cartledge

Poythress, V. S. (1980), Linguistic and sociological analyses of modern tongues-speaking: their contribution and limitations, *Westminster Theological Journal*, 42, 367–388.

Samarin, W. J. (1969), Glossolalia as learned behaviour, *Canadian Journal of Theology*, 15, 60–4.

Samarin, W. J. (1972), *Tongues of Men and of Angels*, New York, Macmillan.

Samarin, W. J. (1973), Glossolalia as regressive speech, *Language and Speech*, 16, 77–89.

Scotland, N. (1994), *Charismatics and the Next Millennium: Do They Have a Future?* London, Hodder and Stoughton.

Silverman, D. (1993), *Interpreting Qualitative Data: Methods for Analysing Talk, Text and Interaction*, London, Sage.

Stake, R. E. (1995), *The Art of Case Study Research*, London, Sage.

Turner, M. (1996), *The Holy Spirit and Spiritual Gifts Then and Now*, Carlisle, Paternoster Press.

Walker, A. (1985), *Restoring the Kingdom: The Radical Christianity of the House Church Movement*, London, Hodder and Stoughton.

Yin, R. K. (1984), *Case Study Research: Design and Methods*, London, Sage.

Yin, R. K. (1993), *Applications of Case Study Research*, London, Sage.

10

Pentecostalism: Charismata and Church Growth

William K. Kay

Introduction

T he phenomenal growth of the Pentecostal movement
around the world since the start of the twentieth century
is reflected in the statistics presented in the *World Christian
Encyclopedia* (Barrett, 1982) and updated in Barrett (1988).
These statistics distinguish between Pentecostalism, the charismatic movement and Third Wavers (mainstream church
renewal), but this distinction is more concerned with ecclesiology than with spiritual experience, as Barrett in his summar-
ization is keen to acknowledge. Altogether these three groups
are projected to amount to 28.6 per cent of the world's church-
member Christians by the year 2000, a percentage that has risen
from a mere 6.4 per cent in 1970.

Clearly, the reasons for this growth are important in a
variety of ways. Few, if any, identifiable groups have grown in
so many different parts of the world at the same rate or reached
such proportions. There were 463 million Pentecostals,
charismatics and Third Wavers in 1995 (Synan, 1997) and
almost none in 1900. Without the support of a powerful state
machinery (as was the case with Marxist or Maoist ideology) it
is necessary to look for another set of dynamics to account for
this extraordinary occurrence.

There is an extensive literature on church growth (Gibbs,

1981; McGavran, 1955, 1959, 1970, 1983; Wagner, 1976, 1984, 1987) that argues for compatibility between congregation and surrounding community and for the authoritative and participatory leadership of the minister. Wagner (1984, p. 169) stresses particularly the need for full-time ministers to be leaders and equippers and for the congregation to be followers and lay ministers. The minister teaches and empowers the congregation so that it becomes a ministering entity. This literature on church growth makes use of statistics only to the extent that they illustrate general trends but, in the main, it is not based on survey data or strictly social science methods.

The approach advocated here is to look at the *defining theological characteristics* of Pentecostalism (using the term to cover all three groups) and to relate these to the growth of individual congregations. This approach has the merit of taking the self-understanding of Pentecostalism seriously and, at the same time, of permitting a linkage between theology and sociologically measurable outcomes. Such an approach, moreover, has valuable historiographical applications (Kay, 1992). Pentecostalism's defining theological characteristic is speaking with tongues (glossolalia), understood as a *charisma* or gift of divine grace (Horton, 1934; Gee, 1949, 1967; Carter, 1968; Hollenweger, 1972; Horton, 1976; Cartwright, 1986; Kay, 1989; McGee, 1991; Oss, 1996). All the main Pentecostal groups have constructed a doctrinal position in which glossolalia is intimately associated with the Holy Spirit, usually by way of a crisis experience, and many see glossolalia as the 'gateway' to other charismata. All the main Pentecostal groups expect their ministers to endorse their denomination's doctrinal position with respect to the Holy Spirit, and some require ministers to sign an agreement form annually.

This study builds on and extends the work of Margaret Poloma (1989). Using sociological theory and empirical methods, she studied the largest Pentecostal denomination in the United States, Assemblies of God (AG), and set her findings within a basically Weberian realm of discourse. She judged AG to be facing the classic dilemma of new spiritual movements. On the one hand AG, which was founded in 1914 and in 1988 had a membership of 2 million and 10,000 congregations, has reached a position of strength, financial security and recognition within the evangelical community and, on the other hand, it is beset by the dangers of institutionalization, stagnation and decay. To remove these dangers she argues it must return to its original charismatic vitality but, if it does this, the very structures which ensure stability and respectability are put in jeopardy.

After carrying out questionnaire-based congregational and ministerial surveys Poloma (1989, p. 65) argued that 'religious experiences, whether measured by a charismatic experience index, glossolalia alone, or the experience of divine healing, proved to demonstrate positive relationships with high levels of evangelistic activities'. Her thesis links 'religious experience to the institutional success of Assemblies of God' (p. 65). She proposes the mechanism by which this success operates. She presumes a line of causation from the minister to the congregation and from the congregation to the community. If the minister embraces a world-view that makes room for the supernatural, the congregation will learn to do the same. A congregation that is open to the supernatural will be more active in personal religious devotion and evangelism, and will offer more attractive worship services to newcomers.

Her empirical evidence finds correlations at each point in the line of causation. More charismatic ministers have more charismatic congregations. More charismatic congregations stress evangelism. Greater evangelism leads to greater church growth.

Having said this, Poloma is careful to point out that charismatic gifts are not the only factor within this series of equations. The non-rational or affective nature of charismatic gifts must be counterbalanced by a rational and orderly framework. Poloma (1989, p. 87) says that 'an affectivity that stresses the supernatural tells only part of the pastoral story. Rational leadership is very much present within Assemblies of God, a leadership that is characterised by a twentieth-century pragmatism'. The marriage between 'this-worldly pragmatism' and 'other-worldly supernaturalism' is the basis for the Weberian dilemma. If pragmatism increases, the charismatic gifts may be buried in routine and lose their power and attractiveness; if the supernaturalism increases there is a danger of subjectivism and institutional fragmentation. Continued progress can only occur when neither of these tendencies predominates.

The present study explores the relationship between church growth and charismata through the eyes of British Pentecostal ministers. This is where Poloma's data began and what her correlations establish. Her negative conclusions linking institutionalization with a reduction of charismata and a lessening of church growth are theoretical glosses based upon her overall interpretation of data comparable with those collected here. The reasons for decline, of course, are more difficult to establish than the reasons for growth since decline may be caused by the absence of certain features rather than the presence of others. It is impossible to obtain correlations between non-existent features of church life and non-attendance at church.

The four charismata included in this study are: public utterance of glossolalia, glossolalic singing, prophecy and dancing in the Spirit. Public utterance of glossolalia would normally be followed by an interpretation, usually coming from the body of the congregation. Public ministerial utterance in tongues therefore serves to develop a rapport between minister and congregation and to prompt the congregation into the exercise of the spiritual gift of interpretation. Prophecy, like interpretation, results in a comprehensible language utterance that is believed to be inspired by the Holy Spirit (Grudem, 1986) and for the 'strengthening, encouragement and comfort' (1 Corinthians 14:3) of all the believers present. Glossolalic singing is normally found in worship and sounds like a plainsong chant, though it is spontaneous. Dancing in the Spirit is rarer and is expressive of joy, triumph and praise. It has the effect of stirring the congregation to emulation.

Method

Sample

The study reported on here makes use of a postal survey by questionnaire among the four main Pentecostal denominations in Britain: the Assemblies of God, Elim Pentecostal Church, Apostolic Church and Church of God. Each of these denominations publishes an annual yearbook listing its ordained clergy. Each distinguishes between ministers who work in the UK and missionaries who work overseas. For the purposes of this study, overseas workers were excluded. All other workers, active, retired, itinerant and pastoral were included.

Although each denomination makes use of a different governmental structure, there are broad similarities between their operations. The distribution and reminder procedure adopted in the case of each denomination was the same and led to a total of 930 usable replies, an overall response rate of 57 per cent.

Respondents were divided between 907 (97.5 per cent) males and 23 (2.5 per cent) females. There were 242 (26 per cent) respondents aged under 39, 586 (63 per cent) aged between 40 and 64, 86 (9 per cent) over 65 years, and 16 of undeclared age. Of the total sample 456 (49 per cent) reported themselves to be 'in sole charge' of one or more congregations. The sample, then, was predominantly male and middle-aged. Almost exactly half worked in a team or itinerant capacity, while the other half worked alone in charge of at least one congregation.

Instrument

In addition to background information about the respondents, the questionnaire asked, 'By what percentage would you judge that your regular congregation has grown in the past 12 months?' and six possible answers were offered: 'none that I know of', '1–5 per cent', '6–10 per cent', '11–20 per cent', '21–30 per cent' and 'more than 30 per cent'. The answers were pre-coded 1–6 so that, for example, in Table 10.2 a mean of 1.5 would imply that about half the ministers had selected the 'none that I know of' option and the other half had selected the '1–5 per cent' option.

The ministers were also asked 'to indicate how often in the past three months *you* have: given public utterance in tongues (glossolalia), sung in tongues (glossolalia), prophesied, danced in the Spirit' (original italics). Ministers were offered five possible answers, 'none', '1–6', '7–12', '13–18' and '19 + '.

Data analysis

Data were analysed by SPSS 6.1 for Windows, Network version (Norussis, 1993).

William K. Kay

Results

Table 10.1 shows the properties of the ministerial charismatic scale that was created using appropriate questionnaire items. The very satisfactory alpha coefficient of 0.61 demonstrates that ministers who are active in one charisma tend to be active in others also.

Table 10.1 Scale of charismatic activity

Activity	Item-rest of test
Minister's public glossolalia	0.2472
Minister's singing in glossolalia	0.4427
Minister's prophecy	0.4575
Minister's dancing in the Spirit	0.4482
Alpha	0.6085

The ministerial charismatic scale was correlated with church growth ($r = 0.24$, $p < .001$) using the whole sample. The positive and significant correlation indicates that charismatically active ministers are those whose churches are growing. A further correlation was calculated for the subset of ministers in sole charge of a congregation ($r = 0.28$, $p < .001$). The second coefficient was higher than the first and this substantiates the connection between charismatically active ministers and church growth since ministers in sole charge of congregations are likely to have a greater impact on their people than those who function as a part of teams.

Having demonstrated the clear correlation between charismatic activity and church growth, Table 10.2 now illustrates the practical implications of this relationship by exploring the incremental growth associated solely with frequency of the minister's prophesying. These statistics demonstrate that, on average, ministers who practised no prophecy recorded a church growth score of 2.35 which might be indicative of growth by 6 per cent or 7 per cent per year. By way of contrast, ministers who practised prophecy more than eighteen times in the past three months recorded a church growth score of 3.35 which might be indicative of growth by 11 per cent or 12 per cent per year.

Table 10.2 Frequency of minister's prophecy in last three months and church growth

Prophetic Frequency	Mean of church growth coding	
	All Ministers	Ministers in sole charge
None	2.35 (n = 156)	2.37 (n = 73)
1–6	2.63 (n = 432)	2.63 (n = 230)
7–12	3.03 (n = 126)	3.23 (n = 82)
13–18	3.33 (n = 39)	3.22 (n = 23)
19 plus	3.35 (n = 52)	3.40 (n = 25)

Discussion

Poloma's positive findings are strikingly substantiated. As ministerial charismatic activity increases, church growth increases. And, also following Poloma, we may assume the direction of causation is from ministerial activity to church growth. What cannot be deduced from these data, however, is the negative conclusion that churches fail to grow when institutionalization threatens charismatic spontaneity. Nor do the data, presented as they are here, show whether it is necessary for all the charismatic gifts to operate in a harmonious fashion or whether only one is sufficient to stimulate the evangelism necessary for growth. The alpha coefficient of Table 10.1 suggests that charismatic gifts operate together, but that is as far as the analysis takes us. Further explorations of this database are necessary to determine whether, paradoxically, charismatic activity may also, in some Pentecostal congregations, be associated with decline and how well correlated the charismatic gifts are with each other.

There are also questions that need to be answered about the sociological function of spiritual gifts on congregational life. We have assumed that they establish a rapport between minister and congregation and provide variety and spontaneity within services. We may also be correct in assuming that some charismatic gifts, for example prophecy, operate to encourage personal evangelism and that this leads directly to church growth. Further explorations of these and similar data are necessary to establish whether the linkage between charismata and church growth is to be found within congregations of all sizes or whether ceiling effects come into force at any point. Another set of questions concerns the linkage between ministerial charismatic activity and congregational charismatic activity. Do congregations become more evangelistic or more charismatic, or both, if their minister is charismatic?

These further explorations stem largely from the issues raised by the McGavran and Wagner literature cited earlier. McGavran and Wagner draw their inspiration from biblical models, though there is evidence that management theory from secular sources has some influence on their thinking. Poloma, by contrast, is influenced by sociological theory, but the two intellectual streams, while they have separate antecedents, flow from a common emphasis on rationality that has its sources at least as far back as the enlightenment of the eighteenth century.

From this wider perspective the disciplines of theology and sociology have common elements and what this paper shows is that there are some questions that can only be answered where theology and sociology work together. The identification of the variables which define Pentecostalism is a *theological* identification, even if it is a theological identification that arises from the self-understanding of Pentecostals. The measurement and analysis of these theological variables takes place within a *sociological* framework and using appropriate statistical techniques. A theological analysis alone would not be able to show that church growth and ministerial charismata are linked. A sociological analysis alone would not be bound to select the relevant theological variables for scrutiny. In this sense, this paper conforms to the canons of both its contributing disciplines and is therefore properly interdisciplinary (Kay and Francis, 1996).

Conclusion

Placed in the wider context of world-wide Pentecostal growth, these data provide social science evidence that points to some of the mechanisms underlying the dynamics of the growth of individual congregations. They suggest that Pentecostal congregations within different denominational settings function in similar ways and that individual ministers who see their congregations grow are, in a theological sense, charismatic individuals.

References

Barrett, D. B. (1982), *World Christian Encyclopedia*, Oxford, Oxford University Press.

Barrett, D. B. (1988), Global statistics, in S. M. Burgess, G. B. McGee, and P. H. Alexander, (eds) (1989), *Dictionary of Pentecostal and Charismatic Movements*, Grand Rapids, Michigan, Regency, pp. 810–29.

Carter, H. (1968), *Spiritual Gifts and their Operation*, Springfield, Missouri, Gospel Publishing House.

Cartwright, D. W. (1986), *The Great Evangelists*, Basingstoke, Marshall Pickering.

Gee, D. (1949), *Concerning Spiritual Gifts*, Springfield, Missouri, Gospel Publishing House.

Gee, D. (1967), *Wind and Flame*, Croydon, Heath Press.

Gibbs, E. (1981), *I Believe in Church Growth*, London, Hodder and Stoughton.

Grudem, W. (1986), *The Gift of Prophecy*, Eastbourne, Kingsway.

Hollenweger, W. J. (1972), *The Pentecostals*, London, SCM Press.

Horton, H. (1934), *The Gifts of the Spirit*, Letchworth, Letchworth Printers.

Horton, S. M. (1976), *What the Bible Teaches about the Holy Spirit*, Springfield, Missouri, Gospel Publishing House.

Kay, W. K. (1989), A History of British Assemblies of God, doctoral dissertation, University of Nottingham, published with minor changes as *Inside Story*, Lifestream/Mattersey Hall Publishing, 1990.

Kay, W. K. (1992), Three Generations On: The Methodology of Pentecostal Historiography, *EPTA Bulletin* 10 (1, 2), 58–70.

Kay, W. K. and Francis, L. J. (1996), *Drift from the Churches*, Cardiff, University of Wales Press.

McGavran, D. (1955), *Bridges of God*, New York, New York, Friendship Press.

McGavran, D. (1959), *How Churches Grow*, New York, New York, Friendship Press.

McGavran, D. (1970), *Understanding Church Growth*, Grand Rapids, Michigan, Eerdmans.

McGavran, D. (1983), *Contemporary Theologies of Mission*, Grand Rapids, Michigan, Baker.

McGee, G. B. (ed.) (1991), *Initial Evidence: Historical and Biblical Perspectives on the Pentecostal Doctrine of Spirit Baptism*, Peabody, Massachusetts, Hendrickson Publishers.

Norussis M. (1993), *SPSS for Windows: Base System User's Guide: Release 6.0*, Chicago, Illinois, SPSS Inc.

Oss, D. A. (1996), A Pentecostal/charismatic view, in W. Grudem (ed.), *Are Miraculous Gifts for Today?* Leicester, IVP, pp. 239–83.

Poloma, M. M. (1989), *The Assemblies of God at the Crossroads: Charisma and Institutional Dilemmas*, Knoxville, Tennessee, The University of Tennessee Press.

Synan, V. (1997), *The Holiness-Pentecostal Tradition: Charismatic Movements in the Twentieth Century*, Grand Rapids, Michigan, Eerdmans.

Wagner, C. P. (1976), *Your Church Can Grow*, Glendale, California, Regal Books.

Wagner, C. P. (1984), *Leading Your Church to Growth*, MARC Europe, British Church Growth Association.

Wagner, C. P. (1987), *Strategies for Church Growth*, MARC, British Church Growth Association.

11

Student Expectations of a Church College

Leslie J. Francis, Mandy Robbins and Mandy Williams-Potter

Introduction

T he church colleges have been providing education in England and Wales for over one hundred and fifty years, and as educational institutions their staff have properly been engaged in teaching, scholarship and research. It is a matter of surprise, therefore, that the institutions themselves have rarely become the subject matter of the disciplines so rigorously pursued within them, apart from providing subject matter for the historians. Russell Grigg's (1998) *History of Trinity College Carmarthen: 1848–1998* is an excellent addition to a long line of college histories, including St Martin's College, Lancaster (Gedge and Louden, 1993), St Paul's and St Mary's Colleges at Cheltenham (More, 1992), Ripon and York St John (McGregor, 1991), Culham College (Naylor and Howat, 1982), Bishop Otter College, Chichester (McGregor, 1981), and King Alfred's College, Winchester (Rose, 1981).

In theory, however, the church colleges could provide the raw material for much innovative work in the social sciences, both testing significant theories and contributing to the colleges' own self-understanding and development. Indeed limited examples exist of such work. In the area of theory testing, students at Trinity College, Carmarthen, have contributed to work on measuring attitudes towards Christianity (Francis, Lewis, Philipchalk, Brown and Lester, 1995), modelling the relationship between religiosity and personality (Francis, 1993a; Francis, Lewis, Brown, Philipchalk and Lester, 1995), testing the relationship between religiosity and happiness (Robbins and Francis, 1996), measuring attitudes towards computers (Francis, 1993b, 1995; Francis and Evans, 1995), testing the influence of gender stereotyping on computer related attitudes (Francis, 1994), modelling the relationship between gender orientation and religion (Francis and Wilcox, 1996), refining new indices of personality assessment (Francis, Brown and Philipchalk, 1992), testing established indices of personality (Francis, 1991; Francis, Philipchalk and Brown, 1991), and examining measures of happiness (Francis, Brown, Lester and Philipchalk, 1998).

In the area of contributing to the college's own self-understanding and development, the major pioneering initiative was undertaken by John D. Gay and his associates in the early 1980s in a wide-ranging enquiry, which included an examination of student attitudes and expectations throughout a number of colleges (Gay, Kay and Perry, 1985; Gay, Kay, Perry and Lazenby, 1985, 1986; Lazenby, Gay and Kay, 1987). In their summary report, Gay, Kay, Perry and Lazenby (1985) draw a profile of the student body in the following terms.

> Students drawn to the colleges tend to be predominantly female (well over twice as many women as men) and middle class (over half of them being from social groups 1 or 2. For most of their families, the present generation represents their first experience of higher education (about three in ten of their fathers are graduates) ... The great majority are aged 20 or less when they come to college. The academic level of undergraduate students on entry is fairly modest – three-quarters of them have A grade levels no higher than the equivalent of three Ds or two Cs.

The summary report goes on to suggest that the level of religious commitment of staff and students 'remains high in comparison with similar groups of people in other walks of life'. According to the data three-quarters of the students described themselves as members of one of the main Christian denominations, one-third say that they attend church services most weeks, and around a quarter describe themselves as having 'strong' or 'total' commitment to Christianity. In their section on student choices and expectations, Gay, Kay, Perry and Lazenby (1985) found that three-quarters of the students were aware that the college was of an Anglican foundation when they applied.

The view that church colleges remain, in any sense, Christian communities which may attract church-related students expecting a distinctive educational environment has been seriously challenged by Edward Norman (1996), who argues as follows: 'Students rarely choose colleges for themselves – they are directed by parents and school teachers. Few opt for voluntary colleges because of their religious affiliations; most decisions are made on the basis of courses offered, and the actual location of the campus.'

Against this background, the aim of the present study was to chart the expectations of the incoming students to Trinity College, Carmarthen, an institution founded by the Anglican Church in 1848, now offering a range of undergraduate and postgraduate provision within the University of Wales. Using standard sociological tools of enquiry, shaped to pursuing matters of theological interest, the study interrogates the extent to which undergraduates currently perceive a church college as a religiously distinctive environment.

Method

In October 1995 and October 1996, some three weeks after the beginning of term, a detailed questionnaire was distributed to all first-year undergraduates at Trinity College. The students were assured of anonymity and confidentiality. From the total intake of 847 undergraduates over these two years, 517 returned thoroughly completed questionnaires, making a response rate of 61 per cent.

Three-quarters of the respondents (74 per cent) were female and 26 per cent were male; 70 per cent were under the age of twenty, 12 per cent were aged twenty or twenty-one, and 18 per cent were aged twenty-two or over; 43 per cent were following the BEd programme, 47 per cent were following BA courses and

11 per cent were following BSc courses; 89 per cent were single.

As well as asking general questions about different aspects of religiosity, the questionnaire included three sets of items which are discussed in the present chapter. The three sets are concerned with the undergraduates' choice of Trinity as a church college, the undergraduates' expectations of a church college, and the undergraduates' understanding of the place of the chapel and chaplaincy in a church college. Each set contained six items. Each item was assessed on a five-point Likert scale ranging from 'agree strongly' and 'agree' through 'not certain' to 'disagree' and 'disagree strongly'. In the present analysis, however, the 'agree strongly' and 'agree' categories have been combined.

Results

Religious identity

Just over one-quarter of the students (27 per cent) claimed no religious affiliation, just one identified as Jewish, and the remaining 73 per cent claimed membership of one of the Christian denominations or sects. Of the Christian churches, the largest group were Anglicans (27 per cent) with Roman Catholics in second place (14 per cent).

In response to somewhat different self-assessments of religiosity, 63 per cent of the undergraduates said that they regarded themselves as 'a religious person'. One in five (19 per cent) attended church at least weekly and more than one in four (28 per cent) prayed at least weekly.

These statistics make it clear that the incoming students to Trinity College are far from being a secular body to whom religion is a matter of irrelevance or indifference.

Coming to Trinity College

Table 11.1 sets out the six questions concerned with the undergraduates' motivation for coming to Trinity College and their initial experience on arrival.

Table 11.1 Coming to Trinity College

	agree %
I knew that Trinity College was a church college before I applied	72
I chose to come to Trinity because it is a church college	7
Trinity College was not my first choice of college	40
I was not sure that I wanted to come to Trinity College	18
During the first week I doubted if I would be happy in Trinity College	30
I feel that Trinity College is too Anglican in its outlook	5

In one sense these statistics provide encouragement for the appreciation of a church college. Nearly three-quarters (72 per cent) of the undergraduates affirmed that they knew that Trinity was a church college before applying. This compares with 76 per cent found by Gay, Kay and Perry (1985) throughout the church colleges. In other words, the situation has not significantly changed over the past decade. The majority of those who apply and accept a place do so in full knowledge that they are coming to a church college. Moreover, once there only a small minority (5 per cent) feel that the college is too Anglican in its outlook. In other words, having arrived, they seem content within a church foundation.

In another sense, however, these statistics are discouraging for the appreciation of a church college. Only 7 per cent of the undergraduates affirmed that they chose to come to Trinity because it is a church college. When Lazenby, Gay and Kay (1987) asked a similar question of Trinity College students during the academic year 1985–86, the figure stood at 11 per cent. Once again the situation has not significantly changed over the past decade.

The fact that the church-related status of Trinity College is so irrelevant to student choice of the college could be interpreted in two ways. One interpretation is that the religious factor is now seen by students to be of no potential significance. Another interpretation is that the practical distinctiveness of the church colleges generally is so poorly profiled and marketed that the potential significance of this issue does not reach salience in the applicants' consciousness. Evidence to help adjudicate between these two interpretations is presented in the following sections.

First, however, it is important to evaluate the under-graduates' more general appreciation of Trinity College. The data demonstrate that 40 per cent did not select the college for their first choice, 18 per cent were not sure that they wanted to come to Trinity College, and 30 per cent were unsure that they would be happy there during the first week of term.

Expectations of a church college

Table 11.2 turns attention to the six questions concerned with the undergraduates' expectations of a church college.

Table 11.2 Expectations of a church college

	agree %
I expected a church college to be a specially caring place	47
I expected a church college to be a specially friendly place	60
I expected a church college to have many Christian students	45
I expected a church college to be conservative in its outlook	18
I expected a church college to have a ban on alcohol	2
I expected a church college to discourage sex outside of marriage	11

These statistics demonstrate that there are many positive ways in which the undergraduates expect a church college to be distinctive. Thus, 60 per cent expected a church college to be a specially friendly place, and 47 per cent expected a church college to be a specially caring place. Nearly half (45 per cent) expected a church college to have many Christian students.

These expectations are consistent with the image that the incoming students are far from being a secular body to whom religion is a matter of irrelevance and indifference. At least around half of the undergraduates expect to find themselves in a Christian community where individuals matter and demon-strate concern one for another.

The expectations which the undergraduates have of this caring Christian community are essentially liberal and permissive. The vast majority (82 per cent) do not expect a church college to be conservative in outlook. Only 2 per cent expect a church college to have a ban on alcohol, while 11 per cent expect a church college to discourage sex outside marriage.

For the majority of incoming undergraduates, therefore, a church college is seen to be a place in which they grow and develop as full citizens of the twenty-first century but with the added benefit of a religiously supportive environment.

The place of chapel and chaplaincy

Table 11.3 focuses on the six questions concerned with the undergraduates' understanding of the place of the chapel and the chaplaincy within a church college. The chapel and chaplaincy have been selected for close examination since these features are clearly identifiable as explicit signs of the Christian tradition, even in a post-Christian or secular context.

Table 11.3 The place of chapel and chaplaincy

	agree %
It is important to me that there is a chapel in the college	30
It is important to me that there is a chaplain in the college	31
I think it is important that there are daily services in the college chapel	54
I find the college chapel a welcoming place	53
I feel the college chapel tries to serve the spiritual needs of all students	54
I feel comfortable within the college chapel environment	39

The statistics show that over half the students hold a positive view of the college chapel. Thus, 53 per cent personally find the college chapel a welcoming place, 54 per cent feel that the college chapel tries to serve the spiritual needs of all students, and 54 per cent think that it is important that there are daily services in the college chapel. While only a handful of students turn up day by day to the services, over half the student body appreciate being part of a community where the presence of God is celebrated in daily worship.

For nearly a third of the students the significance of the chapel and the chaplaincy goes deeper than this. Thus, 30 per cent of the undergraduates say that it is actually important to them that there is a chapel in the college, and 31 per cent say that it is important to them that there is a chaplaincy in the college. Personally 39 per cent feel comfortable within the college chapel environment. These students appear to be looking for something more than simply knowing that they are part of a community where the presence of God is celebrated in daily worship. They wish to know that the chapel and the chaplaincy are available for them as and when they may experience need for these facilities.

Conclusion

Three main conclusions emerge from this study.

First, the data challenge Edward Norman's (1996) empirically unsubstantiated view that students attending a church college bring with them no clear expectations about a religiously distinctive environment. Many students attending Trinity College regard themselves as religious individuals, in whatever sense, who expect to find themselves working among Christian students in a liberally supportive Christian environment in which the presence of God is celebrated through daily worship and where the chapel and the chaplaincy are available to serve the needs of the whole student body.

Second, the data demonstrate that little has changed since the surveys conducted by John D. Gay and his associates, over a decade ago, in the sense that the majority of students knew that they were applying to a church college, but only a handful made the church-related foundation of the institution a decisive factor in their choice to come to Trinity College.

Third, these findings suggest that the major problem facing church colleges at the end of the twentieth century is not that of recruiting students sympathetic to the religious ethos. Rather the problem is that of projecting and marketing a clear image concerning the ways in which a church college may be distinctive precisely because it is a church college. The voices of the incoming undergraduates heard through the present survey suggest one way in which such marketing could be achieved. The church colleges need to make much more use of the positive perceptions of their current students in unashamedly commending the distinctiveness of the church college among those applying for places in higher education, exploiting fully the media of print, video and the internet.

References

Francis, L. J. (1991), The dual nature of the EPQ lie scale among college students in England, *Personality and Individual Differences*, 12, 1255–60.

Francis, L. J. (1993a), Personality and religion among college students in the UK, *Personality and Individual Differences*, 14, 619–22.

Francis, L. J. (1993b), Measuring attitude toward computers among undergraduate college students: the affective domain, *Computers and Education*, 20, 251–5.

Francis, L. J. (1994), The relationship between computer-related attitudes and gender stereotyping of computer use, *Computers in Education*, 22, 283–9.

Francis, L. J. (1995), The measurement of attitudes toward computers among undergraduate students in Wales: the comparison of four scales in relationship to sex, age, personality and religion, in Y. J. Katz (ed.), *Computers in Education: Pedagogical and Psychological Implications*, pp. 85–112, Sofia, Bulgarian Academy of Science.

Francis, L. J., Brown, L.B., Lester, D. and Philipchalk, R. (1998), Happiness as stable extraversion: a cross-cultural examination of the reliability and validity of the Oxford Happiness Inventory among students in the UK, USA, Australia and Canada, *Personality and Individual Differences*, 24, 167–71.

Francis, L. J., Brown, L. B. and Philipchalk, R. (1992), The development of an abbreviated form of the Revised Eysenck Personality Questionnaire (EPQR-A): its use among students in England, Canada, the USA and Australia, *Personality and Individual Differences*, 13, 443–9.

Francis, L. J. and Evans, T. E. (1995), The reliability and validity of the Bath County Computer Attitude Scale, *Journal of Educational Computing Research*, 12, 135–46.

Francis, L. J., Lewis, J. M., Brown, L. B., Philipchalk, R. and Lester, D. (1995), Personality and religion among undergraduate students in the United Kingdom, United States, Australia and Canada, *Journal of Psychology and Christianity*, 14, 250–62.

Francis, L. J., Lewis, J. M., Philipchalk, R., Brown, L. B., and Lester, D. (1995), The internal consistency reliability and construct validity of the Francis scale of attitude toward Christianity (adult) among undergraduate students in the UK, USA, Australia and

Leslie J. Francis, Mandy Robbins and Mandy Williams-Potter

Canada, *Personality and Individual Differences*, 19, 949–53.

Francis, L. J., Philipchalk, R. and Brown, L. B. (1991), The comparability of the short form EPQ-R with the EPQ among students in England, the USA, Canada and Australia, *Personality and Individual Differences*, 12, 1129–32.

Francis, L. J. and Wilcox, C. (1996), Religion and gender orientation, *Personality and Individual Differences*, 20, 119–21.

Gay, J., Kay, B., Perry, G. (1985), *The Future of the Anglican Colleges: The First Year Students*, Abingdon, Culham Educational Foundation.

Gay, J., Kay, B., Perry, G. and Lazenby, D. (1985), *The Future of the Anglican Colleges: The Third Year and PGCE students*, Abingdon, Culham Educational Foundation.

Gay, J., Kay, B., Perry, G. and Lazenby, D. (1986), *The Future of the Anglican Colleges: Final Report of the Church Colleges Research Project*, Abingdon, Culham Educational Foundation.

Gedge, P. S. and Louden, L. M. R. (1993), *S. Martin's College Lancaster 1964–89*, Lancaster, Centre for North-West Regional Studies, University of Lancaster.

Grigg, R. (1998), *History of Trinity College Carmarthen: 1848–1998*, Cardiff, University of Wales Press.

Lazenby, D., Gay, J. and Kay, B. (1987), *Trinity College Carmarthen: A Profile 1985–86*, Abingdon, Culham Educational Foundation.

McGregor, G. P. (1981), *Bishop Otter College: And Policy for Teacher Education 1839–1980*, London, Pembridge Press.

McGregor, G. P. (1991), *A Church College for the 21st Century? 150 Years of Ripon and York St John*, York, University College of Ripon and York St John.

More, C. (1992), *The Training of Teachers 1847–1947: A History of the Church Colleges at Cheltenham*, London, Hambledon Press.

Naylor, L. and Howat, G. (1982), *Culham College History*, Abingdon, Culham Educational Foundation.

Norman, E. (1996), Coping with a crisis of identity, *Church Times*, 14 June, p. 16.

Robbins, M. and Francis, L. J. (1996), Are religious people happier? a study among undergraduates, in L. J. Francis, W. K. Kay and W. S. Campbell (eds), *Research in Religious Education*, pp. 207–17, Leominster, Gracewing.

Rose, M. (1981), *A History of King Alfred's College, Winchester, 1840–1980*, London, Phillimore.

12

Sociology Students and Christianity in a Church College

Bernadette Casey, Neil Casey and Colin Dawson

Introduction

T his chapter reports on research undertaken into the religiosity of sociology students in a Church of England college of higher education. The study emerged from an initial interest in the relationship between sociology, both as a received curriculum and a discipline, and student faith where each discourse would appear to be explaining and seeking to understand the array of social life including, of course, religion itself. We had anecdotal and occasional cases where an avowedly Christian student had evidently found difficulties in reconciling a collision of discourses (an exam answer explaining inequality in terms of God's providence for example), but we were interested in more rigorous evidence which went beyond the classroom. Thus while the interface between sociology and religion as disciplines was investigated, we also sought to acquire data on other aspects of students' faith and views. This follows a similar path to that taken by Mutli (1996) with regard to the relationship between Islamic beliefs and the values of modernization and democracy. In our study a qualitative approach via the collection of religious life-histories allowed interviewees to help set a research agenda and enabled us to ascertain students' *own* accounts of their beliefs, experiences and attitudes.

The research was undertaken in two parts. First, all students

155

on sociology courses in the college were given a survey questionnaire which sought to garner information on various matters including their reasons for coming to the college and their religiosity. The results need not detain us here. Suffice it to say that they were comparable with larger-scale studies in suggesting patterns of continuing religious belief but limited levels of church attendance and membership (see Bruce, 1995; Brierley, 1991; Davie, 1994; Francis, 1989; Levitt, 1996).

The questionnaire was also designed for a second purpose. The aim was to locate a specific group of students: those who described themselves as religious and were willing to be subject to an unstructured interview investigating features of their 'belief experience' and academic experience. We wished to probe their perception of any links or conflicts between academic (particularly sociological) thought and religious belief and practice.

The interviewees were selected from the original sample to whom the questionnaire was administered, and selection was based wholly on two criteria: the stated willingness of respondents to put themselves forward for interview, and the self-definition of respondents as 'Christian' on the question-naire. Out of this, we were able to identify ten sociology students for interview.

The interviews were unstructured, although the interviewer had a 'checklist' of areas deemed relevant to the enquiry. The intention was to allow the interviewees to set the agenda as far as possible. The conversation was framed in terms of a life-history of the interviewee's religious and educational biography which would allow themes to emerge. We wanted to maximize the chance for interviewees to enunciate issues important to them. Such a methodology also implies a number of other things: that the researcher is her/himself at the heart of the process rather than 'outside' it, that there is a commitment to take seriously the subjects' own concerns and lastly, that qualitative data are valued.

This chapter will proceed by identifying some recurrent themes which emerged from the unstructured interview data, including student views on: organized religion and churches; the social image of Christians and Christianity; lifestyle, moral values and being a Christian; and sociology, academic thought and religious belief. The findings are then related to work on changes within religiosity in what has variously been termed high, late, or postmodernity. First, however, something needs to be said about the religious biography of the interviewees.

Religious biography

In the case of religious background, a great deal of divergence and some commonality is evident. All but one of those interviewed reported some degree of religious socialization in their childhood, in a number of denominations and churches, sometimes more than one in the same individual's experience. Most of them reported coming from a family where at least one, and in most cases both, parents were churchgoers. We can only surmise that this experience laid some foundations for subsequent orientations, but from childhood onwards, inter-viewees' biographies in relation to religion were highly divergent.

Interestingly, a number of those interviewed had either switched from the religion in which they were nurtured in favour of another form, or reported a period of time when they 'drifted' from religious attendance and sometimes from faith. This pattern of drift fits with a number of other studies (see for example Toon and Towler, 1983; Levitt, 1996). In Levitt's research women who had changed denomination in adolescence invariably made the change with a friend or sibling of their own age so that the attraction would seem to have been to assert a degree of independence by moving away from more traditional churches which they had attended with family. This may relate to spiritual development and the stage at which individuals come to own their spirituality; student life is a prime example of this metaphorical and often literal leaving of home.

One more qualifying observation needs to be made. It should be stressed that almost all the interviewees seemed to be currently engaging in a process of evaluation of their religious beliefs (although this could be partly explained as an effect of the interviews themselves). In some cases, this meant a confirmation of belief; for others, it seems that a more profound crisis of faith was emerging. How far this is linked to the students' educational stage or the broad influence of academic and sociological perspectives is worthy of further research.

Views on organized religion and churches

Interviewees for the most part were either critical of organized religion or commented on negative experiences within religious groups. Examples include:

> I came back to Britain, all my children had gone to Sunday School with me, I'd gone to church and I came back and went to my local large Church of England church and it was absolutely abominable, it was horrible. They just ignored me, I didn't get spoken to and the vicar was so unfriendly and the average age of people in the church was 70 and I just felt completely out of place. They're just completely out of touch with the real world. (Female, Year 3)

> I went to a Baptist chapel for a year or two ... and found myself dissatisfied with that ... I think the problem was at the time, looking back on it, the culture of the pastor who was taking it – again he was quite an old guy – and he'd been brought up in a very traditional background and I felt he just couldn't identify at all with any kind of issues that might confront me at the time or anything like that. And I didn't like the authoritarianism of it, he would say, 'I'm the captain of the ship, you're the sailors and if you've got any kind of grievances with anything I say on a Sunday morning you don't say them there and then.' (Male, Year 2)

In one or two cases, comments were specifically made about particular styles of worship or individual religious groups. One interviewee recounted a long story about his involvement and subsequent disillusionment with a small Christian fundamentalist group. One anecdote relates to the group's attitude towards alcohol:

> Well, we'd actually stocked up the fridge to be honest with lots of beer and lager and cider and that sort of stuff, to be consumed later on, and we raised this point and – it probably seems very naïve now –

and said 'What's the situation with drinking?' because we knew a lot of people would say it's better if you don't, sort of thing. And they said 'Oh I wouldn't want to risk my salvation by having a pint of beer' – and we weren't actually talking about drunkenness, it was about if you consumed any alcohol whatsoever, it was sulphurous lakes of fire. (Male, Year 2)

What is apparent is a sense of evaluation of religious experience and, in particular, the conflict experienced between being a 'normal' student where a value is placed on freedom, independence, experimentation and escape from convention (both geographically and culturally) and being religious, which may involve a significant emphasis on obedience and self-control.

The social image of Christians and Christianity

The image of Christians came up in the interviews as students talked about life at college and the ways they experienced being Christian within a mixed community. It was fascinating that much of the discussion around the topic was focused on others' perceptions of Christianity (or more accurately, the interviewees' perceptions of those perceptions) and difficulties developing from those perceptions (see also Levitt, 1996). It is possible to identify more than one way in which this general topic was expressed. For example:

I've got my beliefs and obviously they don't believe the same as me so I think well, 'that's their views' . . . I've got close friends who aren't religious and they don't want anything to do with it so I don't try and force it at them . . . sometimes the non-religious ones make fun but nothing we can't handle . . . They say 'Sue will lend you some money because she's a Christian' – stupid things like that. (Female, Year 2)

In another case, a first year student who identified herself as both Christian and religious explained why she did not attend church meetings or Christian Union events in college:

> It just created a barrier and it's really horrible.
> People say 'Oh they go to church' and stuff ...
> There's a sort of thing like, well there is this image
> isn't there? If you go to church you're quiet, you get
> on with your work, but it's not like that ... there's
> this image because when I go (to meetings) I like to
> argue everything and I'm just worried they're going
> to be like, 'If God says this, it's like this.' It just
> seems a lot of people you speak to, they never doubt
> their religion at all. They never question it, they've
> never said to themselves 'Do I agree with it?'
> (Female, Year 1)

This public image of Christians was mentioned more explicitly
by another student:

> I think public opinion of a Christian is someone that
> goes around spouting the Bible every 5 seconds ...
> when I've spoken to people about going to church
> they've said 'Oooh aren't you a good girl' and stuff
> like that. (Female, Year 2)

What is interesting from these responses is that this
particular group of Christian sociology students have handled
their uneasy position between student culture and organized
religion by privatizing or marking off their religious belief and
practice, and by disassociating themselves from others'
perceptions.

Lifestyle, moral values and being a Christian

Although we have identified a somewhat critical or negative
stance taken by our interviewees in relation to some aspects of
religion and have demonstrated ways in which they were able to
put a distance between themselves and what they perceived as a
stereotyped view of Christians, almost all of them nevertheless
claimed an adherence to a lifestyle, or to ways of behaving which
they identified as being congruent with their own personal set of
religious beliefs and values. There were many examples of this
compared with only two students who felt their beliefs did not
significantly affect their lifestyle. In both cases, they had reported

feeling a good deal of disillusion about religion but indicated a belief in God and in an afterlife. The following extracts illustrate both respondents' general approach:

> With the children, I don't throw Christianity down their throat but I don't like them taking God's name in vain. If they come in and go 'Jesus Christ' or 'God', I will pick them up on that ... Religion can be used as a way of guiding you but it doesn't have to be a tool that you live your life through. (Female, Year 3)

> That's the most embarrassing part really. I think it doesn't particularly prevent me or stop me or inhibit me at all ... When I had very entrenched views, I'd try and live this holier than thou kind of life to the extent that I'd collected all these rock'n'roll albums and heavy metal albums as a kid and I had to smash all of those, almost like a public burning, I had to get rid of this satanic music ... As it stands at the moment, rightly or wrongly, religious morals don't encroach on anything I do. (Male, Year 2)

All others interviewed claimed that their religion had a definite impact on their lives and they gave specific examples:

> For me, I try to live a holy life I guess. And that means not doing certain things which perhaps as a student ... I try not to go out and get thoroughly pissed. (Male, Year 2)

> I don't believe in sex before marriage and ... I think stuff like drinking in order to get drunk I don't agree with ... it can lead to all sorts of things that you shouldn't really be getting yourself into. I think it's just leading a general Christian life, trying to follow God's word and if you mess up asking for forgiveness and carrying on again. (Female, Year 1)

> I always think things through and if I say or do anything then – I've always got to say something ...

Bernadette Casey, Neil Casey and Colin Dawson

> I take the sacraments once a month and there's no
> way I'd take them without thinking things through. I
> know that sounds pompous but it's true ... it's so
> true it's a pain, it drags my girlfriend down. (Male,
> Year 2)

It would appear then that there is some evidence of the
translation of moral and religious beliefs into lifestyle, but this
is not uniform.

Sociology, academic thought and religious belief

A specific quest in this research was to assess the impact of
studying sociology on the religious beliefs of students. How far
did sociology, a 'critical' discipline, create problems or tensions
for Christian students? How far did they make connections
between their academic work and their religious beliefs? Did
they perceive there to be contradictions between one system of
thought and another?

The interviews revealed something rather unexpected. It
showed us that, with this sample of students, there was very
little overt connection made between sociology and religious
belief but that, in a more oblique way, doing academic work
could be seen as having an influence on their religious
perspective. In short, students were just as likely to say that
biology, history or another subject had influenced their
thinking, as to say that sociology had done so. Conversely,
sociology, and academic work in general, was sometimes said
to have confirmed rather than contradicted their religious
beliefs. Students displayed a remarkable ability to keep
academic systems of thought quite separate from their
religiosity. The following extracts illustrate quite well, the
variability here. First, an example from the former category.

> But all of those things (sociology, psychology,
> biology) they raise very salient points I think about
> religion in general. It's very difficult to get, certainly
> I could never be a fundamentalist, put it that way,
> for a number of reasons.
> *Interviewer*: So doing these subjects has affected
> your beliefs?

It has, but I would say in many ways it's only reinforced in many aspects, well at least, questions it's partly answered, or partly addressed if not answered, questions I had in the first place ... It's just given me an education and a directive in things I felt in the first place. (Male, Year 2)

These next examples illustrate the separation of faith and academic endeavour:

Things like Marx saying religion is an opium for the people I don't really agree with that ... so you have to take it as their view and not as the truth, they believe one thing and you believe another so I mean, that's the way of life really isn't it? ... You have to take into consideration what they say but you know generally I'll just sort of, you know, write it down and think that's what they believe, that's what I believe. (Female, Year 1).

When you look at religion as an institution it always makes us feel like machines. That's how I feel. I guess I'm quite critical of that, I guess that's because I don't like thinking of myself as a machine ... I guess I've separated my faith from my education which I don't know is a good thing or a bad thing. Some of the stuff in sociology, especially Marx, even Durkheim actually – when it comes to origins and stuff, I do tend to think 'Well, I disagree'. (Male, Year 2)

It's when you do Weber and Durkheim, that's easy. It's when you do the modern stuff ... they're all ... sociology seems to be just an argument on words ... I've got two heads really. You've got to. You've got to be two different people. (Male, Year 2)

This evidence suggests that whilst the experience of college might well provide opportunities for new ways of thinking, for these students it does not necessarily go hand-in-hand with rocking their religious foundations. Most students in this group

were able to take up an academic perspective, even to
understand the arguments put forward by sociological thinkers,
and at the same time to 'bracket' their religious beliefs.

Conclusion

The religious stance of this particular group of sociology
students within a church college would seem appropriate for
younger people experiencing a changed stage of their life and
taking a subject which encourages autobiographical analysis.
However, it would also appear to affirm some aspects of a
postmodern drift within religious life. There is evidence here, in
their evaluative, discerning stance, of religious consumers
searching the shelves for faith products to fit their particular
needs. But it is also apparent in the fragmentation and knowing
separation of religious and other identities: God and Giddens
were consciously compartmentalized.

But it is illustrated most starkly by the familiar distinction
between belief and belonging even where membership of a
particular church might have been a central part of these people's
lives in the past and to which they still aspired, at least in theory.
Organized religion simply did not feel 'right' in the context of
higher education, a sociology degree and student culture.

References

Brierley, P. (1991), *Christian England*, London, MARC Europe.
Bruce, S. (1995), *Religion in Modern Britain*, Oxford, Oxford
University Press.
Davie, G. (1994), *Religion in Britain since 1945: Believing without
Belonging*, Oxford, Blackwell.
Francis, L. J. (1989), Drift from the churches: secondary school
pupils' attitudes towards Christianity, *British Journal of Religious
Education*, 11, 76–86.
Levitt, M. (1996), *'Nice when they are Young': Contemporary
Christianity in Families and Schools*, Aldershot, Avebury.
Mutli, K. (1996), Examining religious beliefs among university
students in Ankara, *British Journal of Sociology*, 47, 353–9.
Toon, R. and Towler, R. (1983), *Religious Research Paper 11:
Conventional Religion and Common Religion in Leeds*, Department of Sociology, University of Leeds.

13

Immanent Faith: Young People in Late Modernity

Sylvia Collins

Introduction

T he approach to faith adopted in this study was based on a
functional definition of religion (see Wallis and Bruce,
1992) which suggests that 'religion' is a meaning system which
integrates an individual's identity and locates his/her existence
in the physical and social world. Since all individuals need such
psychological and social coherence to take part in society, all
'normal' human beings are in some sense 'religious' (Luckmann, 1967; Erikson, 1994; Fowler, 1981; see Cottrell, 1985 for
a critique of this view). This perspective was developed with
reference to Giddens' analysis of trust and self-identity in late
modernity since 'faith almost by definition rests on trust'
(Giddens, 1991, p. 196). Giddens argues that all individuals at
some level have to address four existential questions in order to
secure ontological security, or what Tillich (1962) calls 'the
courage to be'. The answers to these questions rely on the
development of 'basic trust'. Thus, for this study faith was
defined as the organization of trust which affords an individual
ontological security, that is, meaning, hope and purpose. Such
organization involves both process and structure. The process
of faith is the ongoing investment of trust in one or more
referents such that threats to ontological security are kept at
bay. The structure of faith is the organization of referents in

which trust is invested and the meanings which surround them such that the faith process is justified and sustained. Following Giddens, one might say that faith provides a 'protective cocoon' which allows the individual to 'bracket out' existential *angst*. In other words, faith is trusting in someone or something so that the individual's life is given meaning, hope and purpose.

Giddens (1990) suggests that the organization of trust has changed over time. In premodern society, he argues, trust was organized around the local community, kinship, religion and tradition, but late modernity sees trust organized in terms of 'abstract systems' (technical or expert knowledge and symbolic tokens which hold common meaning and so can be exchanged on a global scale) and 'pure relationships' (relationships based on internal reflexivity rather than external traditional norms, which exist for their own sake and only for as long as they are mutually satisfying). This accords with more specific analyses of the secularization process (Wilson, 1982). For example, Luckmann (1967) makes a similar point and suggests themes such as the inner self, social mobility, sexuality and familism take the place of conventional religious ideas in modern society. Insofar as these late modern themes make no reference to a transcendent or supernatural realm and therefore defy 'common sense' understandings of religion, Luckmann refers to them as 'invisible' religious representations.

Given this paradigm, the study addressed the following questions: What role does Christianity retain, if any, for young people's faith? If it has little significance what is their faith based on instead? Are they turning to 'common religions' (Towler, 1974) such as astrology or superstitious practices? Are they investing their faith in science or are they basing their faith on some other themes along the lines of Luckmann's suggestions?

Method

A two-stage research design was adopted. The first part involved developing a structured questionnaire designed to gauge the relevance of Christianity and common religion to young people. The questionnaire comprised closed questions with items relating to religious practice and belief, moral attitudes and influences on faith. Some of the items were taken from the European Values Survey (Ester, Halman and de Moor, 1993, pp. 273–99) and from questionnaires reported by Francis (1982, 1984) and Hornsby-Smith and Lee (1979) so that the results from this study could be compared with other research. This questionnaire was completed by 1090 pupils aged 13 to 16 years during religious education lessons in three mixed-sex comprehensive schools in the South East of England: one Church of England aided school, one Roman Catholic aided school and one non-denominational County school. While the questions were presented in a closed format, the young people were encouraged to make further comment if they wanted to elaborate on their ideas. However, even with comments questionnaires of this sort are limited in the 'depth' of information they can provide. The second stage of the research was designed to deal with this limitation.

Using the statistical technique of factor analysis (Child, 1970) nineteen items were selected from the questionnaire and used to construct a Christian religiosity (CR) scale. A CR score was then calculated for each individual which fell between 1.00 and 5.00. Scores on this scale were then employed to divide the sample into three groups: pupils with a strong commitment to Christianity (high CR scores), pupils with a moderate degree of commitment to Christianity (medium CR scores), and pupils for whom Christianity had little or no significance (low CR score). Four individuals (two boys and two girls) ranked top, middle and bottom in the range of Year 10 scores for each school were then selected for follow-up semi-structured interviews on a one-to-one basis (a total of 36 youngsters aged 15 and 16). During the interviews the young people were asked about a wide range of topics relating to the self, personal values, beliefs, influences on belief, social goals and personal morality. The interviews were designed to allow the interviewees to talk about things which were important to them rather than have views imposed on them. The interviews were then analysed by paying attention to emergent themes such that 'invisible' religious representations could be identified.

Results

Table 13.1 sets out some of the results derived from the survey data. One of the most salient features from this table is the

Table 13.1 Young people's beliefs: overview

	Agree %	Not certain %	Disagree %
It is comforting at times to believe there is a God	60	20	20
Heaven is just an imaginary place	15	43	42
Hell is a real place	22	46	32
The Devil is just an imaginary person	26	45	29
I believe in my horoscope	32	25	43
There is really no such thing as luck	15	22	63
When people die they come back to life again as someone or something else	20	49	31
One day everything will be explained by science	30	37	33
God really did make the world in six days and rested on the seventh	18	46	36

degree of uncertainty many of the young people expressed in relation to their beliefs. This accords very much with a study by Martin and Pluck (1977).

Table 13.2 compares the young people in the different CR score groups. The data indicated that low scorers were more likely than the other youngsters to reject items relating to any form of supernatural/transcendent reality, and locate existence only in the material world accessible to scientific investigation and understanding. The interviews suggested such a response was based on the youngsters' perception of religion as irrational and irrelevant to their own lives. They found aspects of Christian teaching, such as Bible stories about miracles and the creation of the universe, irreconcilable with their 'scientific' understanding of the world and, therefore, were inclined to feel that the *whole* Christian faith could be dismissed on the grounds of implausibility. Similarly, common religious beliefs were rejected (though to a lesser extent than Christianity) insofar as they were also incompatible with a rational materialistic framework of belief. The transcendent was

Table 13.2 Young people's beliefs by Christian religiosity group

	High CR Agree %	Medium CR Agree %	Low CR Agree %
It is comforting at times to believe there is a God	97	70	19
Heaven is just an imaginary place	2	7	41
Hell is a real place	57	16	15
The Devil is just an imaginary person	8	24	40
I believe in my horoscope	15	36	34
There is really no such thing as luck	24	10	20
When people die they come back to life again as someone or something else	13	23	17
One day everything will be explained by science	8	29	44
God really did make the world in six days and rested on the seventh	66	11	3

regarded as irrelevant in that the youngsters saw a mismatch between the taught concepts and personal experience. For example, these teenagers knew that the Christian God was supposed to do, and be, good, but their own and other people's experiences of suffering testified otherwise. They made no attempt to try and understand these experiences through a Christian interpretation of good and evil. Likewise, the low-scoring youngsters found common religious beliefs and practices irrelevant since when they had tried them they had been ineffective. In accordance with Giddens' (1991) analysis, the interviews indicated that the high level of belief in luck amongst these teenagers related more to an awareness of the contingent nature of late modernity and levels of risk than to notions of 'fate' or 'Fortuna'. So, for instance, the majority of interviewees did not think luck could be manipulated through superstitious practices.

The majority of young people scored in the medium range of

the CR scale. This group of teenagers were characterized in particular by the uncertainty of their belief. Where they were prepared to state an opinion on the items they tended to be more open to a transcendent reality than the low CR scorers, but were less inclined to accept Christian beliefs and more open to common religion (horoscopes, luck, reincarnation) than the high scorers. The medium scorers implied a degree of nominalism could be attached to their statements of belief since they did not want to dismiss Christian or common religious beliefs out of hand but neither did they want to commit themselves to them. In other words, they retained in the back of their minds an awareness of an 'X factor' just in case there was some truth in a transcendent reality, but they did not allow such ideas to affect their lifestyle in any significant way. In this respect they acted as 'consumers', selecting from a range of beliefs and using them as and when they felt the need to. Their understanding of these religious beliefs therefore tended to be decontextualized and subjectively reinterpreted to make them more appealing or appropriate to their personal circumstances.

The high scorers were inclined to accept conventional Christian ideas rather than common religious beliefs or materialistic rationality expressed through science, both of which could potentially be regarded as a threat to their Christian views. These youngsters explained that the most important aspects of Christianity for them lay in their intimate, personal relationship with God. God was regarded as their guide and helper. Most important of all, God was their trusted confidant and friend. Day and May (1991) report similar findings amongst teenagers. These young people derived their meaning, purpose and hope from their Christian faith. Difficult circumstances were understood within a Christian context as being in God's will and therefore having a purpose, or alternatively were the actions of the Devil and therefore to be overcome with God's superior power. Their Christian faith gave them a hope and purpose in life in that they wanted to serve God and ultimately go to heaven at the point of death.

The above results give an indication of the young people's beliefs in relation to various predefined categories. The interview data were then analysed further to find out if there were any signs of invisible religious representations. In this respect the interviewees made it clear that ultimately the things that were most important to them were family, close friends, self-realization and personal happiness. Family and close friends were trustworthy individuals valued for the support (economic, moral and emotional) they gave to the youngsters, and the sense of belonging that they bestowed on the young person in being part of an intimate social network. Family and close friends also provided the young people with a positive sense of self. That is not to say, however, that all the interviewees came from secure family backgrounds; indeed for some their family relationships were very difficult. Nevertheless, all the young people mentioned at least one family member or close friend who would accept them for 'who they are' and who helped them have the 'courage to be'. Self-realization through achievement (academic, sporting and social) and establishing personal autonomy also gave the young people a positive self-identity and so was important for their ontological security.

Discussion

What do the above results tell us about young people's faith in late modernity? While many young people are aware of Christian and common religious beliefs, their understanding of them was too uncertain to form the basis of faith for the majority of young people, and their understanding of science had for many undermined the plausibility of a transcendent reality. Science itself, however, was also unsuitable as a basis of faith. It could provide the young person with a mechanical understanding of the world but it did not provide a purpose and hope for life. Faith for the young people in this study was therefore mainly organized reflexively around family, close friends and the self. Family and close friends were the faith referents which located the youngster in their world and provided a source of happiness. This faith relationship was reciprocal in that the young person was in turn a referent for the faith of family members and close friends. The self was understood in relation to these significant others and also reflexively constructed and understood in the process of self-realization. Autonomy and authenticity were therefore important. Meaning was established in relation to family/close friends, but it nevertheless was the responsibility of the individual him/herself to construct his/her meanings and establish his/her own hope and purpose for life – there was no necessary recourse to an external absolute authority. Family/close friends and the reflexive self together formed the structure of faith and provided the individual with the 'protective cocoon' for ontological security. A hope and purpose for life was defined in terms of achieving personal happiness (spending time with family/close friends, achievement in a chosen field of interest) and helping others maintain their ontological security through the reciprocal exchange of support and care. The moral basis of social life was then understood as engaging in actions which help maintain the bonds of trust between individuals such that the faith structure could be sustained. Insofar as this faith was internally referential and did not have to locate itself in a transcendent reality, it could be described as 'immanent faith'.

Given that faith was immanent, why did the majority of young people in this study refuse to reject Christianity and common religious beliefs outright? From the interviews it seems that 'customary Christianity' (Hornsby-Smith, 1991) and common religion remain important to the young people in that they are selectively utilized to gain 'information' about the self and/or others which could be used in the reflexive process of immanent faith; they also provide a temporary means of strengthening the 'protective cocoon' when it is under threat. So, for example, a young person might look to the horoscope to provide him/her with information about the long-term future of a relationship and use that to decide whether or not it is worth investing time and emotional effort in. Or if a family member dies the youngster may turn to ideas of heaven or reincarnation as a source of existential comfort. These transcendent referents for the most part, however, are only of transitory relevance and not a permanent feature of the faith structure. Once the bonds of trust in the immanent structure have re-established their strength the transcendent referents can be set aside until they are required at another time.

The exceptions to this were the youngsters with high CR scores. For these young people the transcendent referent was an integral part of their faith structure and hence their faith could be called 'transcendent faith'. The relationships of immanent faith were interpreted in relation to the transcendent reality.

172

However, the transcendent was also based on the immanent faith structure. In all the cases of strong Christian commitment the youngsters had a family member and/or close friend who shared their Christian faith. This was important since they provided what Berger (1969) calls a 'plausibility structure'. In other words, transcendent faith is rooted in immanent faith and is hard to sustain without it. The data from this study confirmed in this respect the importance of groups which afforded the young people close relationships with other Christians, such as Christian Unions and church youth groups. It also suggests that if parents want their children to adopt a Christian faith it will help if they adopt an explicitly Christian faith themselves. Failure to do so weakens the bonds between the transcendent referent and immanent faith; consequently the transcendent is likely to be reduced to the transitory importance of customary religion.

Conclusion

On the basis of this research, therefore, it seems that for the majority of young people faith is immanent, that is faith is organized around family, close friends and the reflexive self. Christianity and common religion only have transitory signifi-cance in supporting this immanent faith structure from time to time; for most young people they do not form a permanent part of the faith structure themselves. This conclusion accords with Luckmann's suggested themes of invisible religion. There is also some resonance with Giddens' description of the organization of trust in late modernity in terms of the reflexive nature of the organization of faith. Abstract systems or science, however, hold little ultimate relevance for the young people. Looking to the future the increased occurrence of family breakdown can be seen as potentially damaging to the faith structure (see Robinson, 1994). Moreover, if relationships are to be characterized more in terms of 'pure relationships' which are inherently unstable we might expect to see an increased interest in the transcendent referents of customary and common religion as we enter the twenty-first century. However, insofar as these referents are only used to shore up the immanent faith structure, this does not indicate a renewed commitment to the transcendent realm, but rather suggests the further breakdown of faith in late modernity.

Sylvia Collins

References

Berger, P. L. (1969), *The Social Reality of Religion*, London, Faber & Faber.

Child, D. (1970), *The Essentials of Factor Analysis*, London, Holt, Rinehart & Winston.

Cottrell, M. (1985), *Secular Beliefs in Contemporary Society*, Unpublished DPhil dissertation, University of Oxford.

Day, D. and May, P. (1991), *Teenage Beliefs*, Oxford, Lion.

Erikson, E. H. (1994), *Identity and the Life Cycle*, New York, Norton.

Ester, P., Halman, L. and de Moor, R. (1993), *The Individualizing Society: Value Change in Europe and North America*, Tilburg, Tilburg University Press.

Fowler, J. W. (1981), *Stages of Faith: The Psychology of Human Development and the Quest for Meaning*, San Francisco, Harper & Row.

Francis, L. J. (1982), *Youth in Transit*, London, Gower.

Francis, L. J. (1984), *Teenagers and the Church: A Profile of Church-going Youth in the 1980s*, London, Collins Liturgical Publications.

Giddens, A. (1990), *The Consequences of Modernity*, Cambridge, Polity Press.

Giddens, A. (1991), *Modernity and Self-Identity: Self and Society in the Late Modern Age*, Cambridge, Polity Press.

Hornsby-Smith, M. P. (1991), *Roman Catholic Beliefs in England*, Cambridge, Cambridge University Press.

Hornsby-Smith, M. P. and Lee, R M. (1979), *Roman Catholic Opinion: A Study of Roman Catholics in England and Wales in the 1970s*, Guildford, University of Surrey.

Luckmann, T. (1967), *The Invisible Religion*, London, Collier-Macmillan.

Martin, B. and Pluck, R. (1977), *Young People's Beliefs*, London, General Synod Board of Education.

Robinson, M. (1994), *The Faith of the Unbeliever*, Crowborough, Monarch Publications.

Tillich, P. (1962), *The Courage to Be*, London, Fontana.

Towler, R. (1974), *Homo Religiosus*, London, Constable.

Wallis, R. and Bruce, S. (1992), Secularisation: the orthodox model, in S. Bruce (ed.), *Religion and Modernization: sociologists and historians debate the secularization thesis*, pp. 8–30, Oxford, Clarendon Press.

Wilson, B. (1982), *Religion in Sociological Perspective*, Oxford, Oxford University Press.

14

Church Leaving in the Late Twentieth Century: Eschewing the Double Life

Philip Richter

Introduction

T he Church Leaving Research Project is currently yielding important new data on the factors involved when people discontinue their participation in churches. The project has focused on Anglican, Methodist, Roman Catholic and New Church leavers. By definition, church leavers are not the easiest people to contact. Unlike churchgoers they do not congregate on Sundays with other like-minded people! We decided to use a combination of qualitative and quantitative research methods. Both approaches have their own strengths and weaknesses: the qualitative approach yields much richer and more nuanced data and avoids imposing preconceived categories on the material, but lacks generalizability; the quantitative approach provides a good general overview, but lacks fine detail. In the event, we decided to capitalize on the strengths of both approaches.

The first phase of the research adopted a qualitative approach, involving a series of 33 in-depth interviews with church leavers and clergy. On the basis of the themes that crystallized from these interviews we were able to develop and refine the questionnaires used in the next phase of the research. In the second phase we adopted a quantitative approach, identifying a sample of 800 church leavers in the population at large by means of a random telephone survey and inviting their completion of an extensive postal questionnaire. This yielded a response rate of 52 per cent.

Using data from the Church Leaving Research Project, Richter and Francis (1998) identified eight broad categories of church leaving. In the present analysis I plan to concentrate on just one of these categories, styled as 'personal authenticity'. In particular, I intend to explore the extent to which searching for personal authenticity on the part of church leavers may be culturally specific, as Wade Clark Roof (1993) has proposed, in his recent study of Baby Boomers, *A Generation of Seekers*.

'I was just going through the motions', 'I was pretending to be someone I wasn't', 'I was living a double life', a number of our interviewees confessed. Alison Matthews, a social worker and Catholic leaver in her twenties, told how she had decided that, 'I couldn't carry on going to church in this regular way ... or months I'd been going to church just out of habit ... I would have to stop going to Mass.' Arron Coates, another young Catholic leaver, a postgraduate student, said, 'I used to make a thing of going and sitting down the front and (participating) very loudly, and then, whenever there's a (liturgical) response, I'm there bellowing, and I thought, "God, why?", because I don't enjoy that, I just want to go and pray in my own little way.' The desire to avoid personal hypocrisy was a frequent motive for our interviewees.

The Baby Boomer generation

In the 1960s and 1970s commentators began to recognize that teenagers were not only leaving the church for time-old reasons, such as adolescent rebellion, but also because of sea-changes in cultural values. If we follow Roof's definition of Baby Boomers, as anyone born between 1946 and 1964 then Baby Boomers were exposed during their most formative years to immense cultural upheavals, such as new musical forms, extensive illicit drug taking, the permissive society, the greater availability of higher education, intense political idealism and unrest, and the growth of new religious movements. Even those who did not become 'flower people' or go to Woodstock or demonstrate in Grosvenor Square were affected by the 'counter-cultural' values of the Baby Boom generation. American youngsters dropped out of church in proportionately greater numbers than before (Roof, 1993, p. 56), those most affected by the value-shifts are least likely to have returned to church (Roof, 1993, p. 171). Baby Boomers have a distinct generational outlook on life, moulded by the events of their late adolescence and early adulthood. After the Baby Boomers came the Baby Busters, born in the years up to 1981, now making up half the UK adult population (Ritchie, 1995, p. 147), and sometimes called Generation X, following Douglas Coupland's (1992) book of the same name. They are a distinctive generation but, as far as the themes I shall be looking at in this chapter are concerned, they are not dissimilar from their predecessors. I shall now map seven of the most significant of the Baby Boomers' new values, many of which, as I have said, are shared with Busters. I shall be focusing on their quest for personal authenticity, whilst offering a glimpse of the wider constellation of values within which this is set.

The first value concerns *prioritization of experience*. Experience takes priority over beliefs for Boomers. In their formative years inherited cultural and religious 'certainties' were jettisoned in favour of authentically 'living in the present moment'. Inspired by the existentialist call to break free from the crowd, from social conditioning and from the fetters of the past they were to have the courage to live truly free, authentic and autonomous lives. Interest in the transcendent was not abandoned, but institutional religion was written off by many as too staid and fossilized. They wanted something that would fit them, rather than something into which they would have to fit. The search was on for 'direct, inward and present' (Troeltsch, 1931, p. 730) self-actualizing spiritual experience, probably best described as 'mystical' in nature, whether it be knowing God or getting in touch with one's true self. It was important to free the human spirit from potentially stifling social structures and conventions.

The premium placed by Boomers on experience underlay ex-New Church leader, Russell Briggs', rejection and leaving of the church as 'redundant': 'Just as the Jewish faith was made obsolete by the church, so the church will be made obsolete by individual experience' he claimed. Alison Matthews had concluded that religious experience was more important than orthodox belief and practice on her part:

177

It doesn't matter how we pray, so long as we pray from the heart. And it really doesn't matter whether we believe in Jesus, or whether we worship God through Jesus, or through some other ways, so long as it's totally genuine. That's what's important to God ... Following my heart and following God is really what the whole reason for my leaving was about.

She had stopped her churchgoing for the sake of her own personal authenticity. She could have continued attending Mass but 'it wouldn't be completely from the heart, and to me that's not good enough'.

The second value concerns *quest for personal authenticity*. Personal authenticity was also important to Arron Coates, who rejected the mechanistic nature of much Catholic worship. People were simply conditioned to be there, he claimed: 'Because it's Sunday ... they've got to go to church, so they sit at the back, they mumble through a few things, they give money whenever a basket is passed under their nose, and as soon as (the priest) says, "Go in the name of God", they're out!' Arron appreciated the sacrament of confession 'because it's not something that you're ever conditioned to do ... I go to confession when I really feel I should actually go'. Deborah Clarke, an ex-Anglican Boomer, spoke of her determination to avoid making the same mistake as her (pre-Boomer) Roman Catholic mother who, thanks to a convent education, had simply been conditioned into accepting her faith without question and, in the process, had been less than true to herself. As Deborah put it: 'I don't think *she* would (ever) presume to say, "And what about *me* in all of this?"' One suspects that, were it not for their strong desire for personal authenticity, some church leavers would have found it easier to remain and continue 'going through the motions'. Samuel Hartley left in order to resolve his sense of hypocrisy over leading what he perceived as a 'double life', as a secretly homosexual Catholic: 'Whenever I went into a church and prayed or went to Mass I had this feeling that I was hiding part of myself.' The desire to avoid personal hypocrisy was a frequent motive for our interviewees.

The third value concerns *commitment to self-fulfilment*. The individual and his or her choices is a central focus for Boomers. Raised in the 'never had it so good' era, they were brought up in a period of untold affluence and soaring expectations. Children were encouraged to express themselves and to believe 'that somehow sheer abundance would nurture them' (Roof, 1993, p. 43). Relative economic security fostered 'post-materialist' values. Instead of the struggle to survive people could now focus on the well-being of the self and the search for meaning. The virtue of self-denial gave way to the new ethic of self-fulfilment. It was important to 'fulfil one's potential' and to have heightened self-knowledge. Life was for growing as a person and for achieving 'quality of life', often facilitated by various kinds of psychological therapy. Although the economic optimism of their childhood later gave way to recession and, for many, negative equity, Baby Boomers still place a very high premium on the growth of the self: they prefer churches in which spiritual growth is not an optional extra.

Diversity of choice has been an important feature of the Baby Boom generation, in consumption, media viewing and especially lifestyle. Religion is a matter of 'preference' and pluralism is highly valued. 'Pre-packaged' religion is often treated with suspicion. Commentators have coined the term 'pick-and-mix spirituality' to describe the fluidity of Boomers' allegiances and the way in which they happily select and combine aspects of various religious traditions.

The fourth value concerns *exaltation of individual choice*. Our interviewees often spoke of their churchgoing as a matter of individual choice. Arron Coates told us: 'It's my choice to go, and there's no point in going half-heartedly.' Alison Matthews believed that 'people need to find their own way' to God: 'What works for one person doesn't work for another, and what will lead one person to God will drive another from him ... People have to find their own paths to God, if that's what they want to do.' Her path had taken her beyond Christianity and she had made an important discovery:

> I was concerned about whether Catholicism was the right way, or Christianity was the right way to worship God, or whether the Ba'hai Faith had all the answers, or whether Buddhism had all the answers, and all these things I was looking into, [but] I've

come to the realisation that whatever God is, God is something far greater and far more wise than something that would be at all worried about how we pray to him, or how we love him.

Donald Harper, an ex-Catholic Boomer, spoke of his agnosticism about the God of the Christian tradition, which is only 'one of a number of ways'. He had a 'growing conviction that religion is an expression primarily of the *human* search for the Other, God, whatever'. He told us: 'I find no problem about (the notion of) unknowable realities, mysteries, "God" if you want to call it that, but ... religion [is] more than the Christian religion.'

The fifth value concerns *attraction to spiritual questing*. Whilst 'religion' was frequently a word with negative associations, 'spirituality' was a term that appealed to many of our Boomer and Buster interviewees. 'The trouble with the church,' Peter Kendall claimed, 'is that it ... nowhere goes to the root of people's deep, deep spirituality. They're not equipped to deal with a new restlessness that people are feeling. It's an end of the millennium restlessness. It's a feeling that the materialism and the way that we've gone in the last thousand years has got to change into a new form of spirituality ... that relates you to the universe, the cosmos.' Interestingly, given his Boomer background, he now criticized 'the 60s Revolution' and 'twentieth-century existential philosophy' as too 'person-centred' and 'too much to do with constructing your own realities'. His spiritual search beyond the church had taught him that the human person is 'part of something which is much, much, much, infinitely, much greater than we are individually'. Leavers tend to use open, questing metaphors to describe their spiritual journey. Deborah Clarke spoke of going on 'a *journey*, a *quest* ... away from the church'. Others spoke of still being on a *pilgrimage* or a *search*. Alison Matthews claimed: 'I'm still searching, I'm still working towards something.'

Postmodern 'pick-and-mix' spirituality was not always acceptable to our interviewees. Suzanne O'Leary, a student in Northern Ireland, claimed that having your 'own individual religion' wouldn't 'really work' there. In Northern Ireland a person's religion is also an important badge of cultural identity. Madeleine, one of our other Northern Irish interviewees, was tempted to pick and choose within her Catholicism but concluded that it would be 'very hypocritical'. The value shifts we are describing in this chapter have, not surprisingly, also spawned counter-reactions. Fundamentalist religion and conservative churches have capitalized on people's unwillingness to live with too much uncertainty.

The sixth value concerns *espousal of alternative lifestyles*. Boomers regard lifestyle as a matter of personal choice and are extremely tolerant of others' different lifestyles. The 'new morality' of the permissive society represented a seachange from the moral values of their parents' generation. Boomers sought independence from the old moral authorities and preferred to make more spontaneous and intuitive decisions about the way they led their lives. It is true that Boomers have now become somewhat more conservative in their attitudes, but tolerance and respect for difference remain key characteristics (Roof, 1993, p. 45), as does the premium placed on individual autonomy.

One of the reasons why some people leave churches is their fear, or their experience, of being rejected because their lifestyle is in some way unconventional. They conclude that such things as having sex outside marriage, taking illegal drugs, or being a practising homosexual or lesbian are incompatible with continued church belonging. As an Anglican vicar we interviewed put it: 'They feel the church isn't the place for them anymore, because I think they feel they've broken the rules.' For Matthew Williams, his Bohemian 'quite wild' lifestyle as an art student in 1977, led to him leaving church: 'Somehow there was a contradiction between being an artist and a Christian.' Samuel Hartley, a young gay Catholic leaver, started to distance himself from the church because of his fear of how the church would react were he to 'come out': 'I felt that if I'd gone in there and told people, "This is who I am, and this is what I do", that the powers that be, or the priest, would have said, "Well, sorry, mate, you can't really take communion, you can't do this" and it was easier just not to bother them (and) to go my own way.' He acknowledged, however, that 'It was my own perception – it may not have been the case.' Congregations might, one hopes, be much less judgemental, in practice, than leavers fear. It is Roman Catholics who are perhaps the most acutely aware of the potential disparity between their own individual morality and that officially sanctioned by their church.

The seventh value concerns *nascent connectedness*. In many respects the so-called 'Me' generation of the Baby Boomers has developed and matured. Preoccupation with self has given way to a greater sense of connectedness with others. Deborah Clarke had recognized the tension between living 'most deeply in yourself' and living 'most deeply in community' and confessed: 'Maybe I'm swinging too hard onto one side at the moment.' Boomers have discovered that commitment to collective organizations, such as churches, can enhance the self and need not stifle it. Genuine self-fulfilment is increasingly recognized as involving 'the cultivation of shared meanings' and 'the sharing of lives' (Roof, 1993, p. 246). It has been claimed that Baby Boomers are 'figuring out what to give themselves to and where to place their energies' (Roof, 1993, p. 185). They are willing to commit themselves but this must be on their own terms. Commitment must be good for the self and its growth, as well as involving the giving of themselves.

The questionnaire findings

We turn now to an analysis of our quantitative survey which we undertook to test our qualitative findings. The questionnaire drew references from a number of existing surveys including Roof (1993), Roof and Johnson (1993) and Hoge (1981). Specifically in this analysis we tested whether there were significant differences between the types of reasons for church leaving given by under 50 year-olds (Boomers and Busters) and those given by people aged 50 and over. Of the total database, 59 per cent of the respondents were under 50 and 41 per cent were aged 50 or over.

On the basis of our interviews and literature review we made the following five predictions which could be tested from the available data. We predicted that those under the age of 50 were more likely to have become church leavers for the following reasons: because they wished to assert their personal authenticity; because they perceived their lifestyle as incompatible with continued church membership; because they were attracted by religious questing and by religious pluralism; because they felt disillusioned by what they saw of other churchgoers; because they felt alienated by religious hypocrisy. Four items were selected from the questionnaire data to illustrate each of these five reasons. We then compared the percentage of people aged under 50 and the percentage of people aged 50 or over who assented to each of these items. Statistical significance between the two groups was computed by means of the chi square test. The findings are summarized in Table 14.1. These data demonstrate that our predictions were generally confirmed.

Table 14.1 Reasons for church leaving by age group

	under 50 %	50 and over %	p <
Personal authenticity			
My churchgoing was hypocritical	37	15	.001
I was going to church for the wrong reasons	44	24	.001
I could not keep going to church and be true to myself	39	26	.01
I wanted to stop pretending to be someone I was not	24	12	.01
Incompatible lifestyle			
I felt my lifestyle was not compatible with participation in the church	47	25	.001
I felt my values were not compatible with participation in the church	44	27	.001
I was taking (illegal) drugs	8	1	.01
I was having sex outside marriage	26	7	.001
Religious pluralism and quest			
It was increasingly difficult to believe Christianity is the only true faith	57	46	.05
I believed that all great religions are equally good and true	42	49	NS
I wanted to follow my own spiritual quest, without religious institutions	41	28	.05
People have God within them, so churches aren't really necessary	44	33	.05
Disillusionment			
I was disillusioned by churchgoers' racism	27	15	.01

	under 50 %	50 and over %	p <
I was disillusioned by churchgoers' attitudes to women	37	15	.001
I was disillusioned by churchgoers' attitudes to homosexuals	38	17	.001
I was disillusioned by churchgoers' attitudes to lesbians	38	17	.001
Rejecting hypocrisy			
The church had become too much like other institutions, losing the spirit of true religion	33	27	NS
I disliked the hypocrisy I saw in other churchgoers	53	34	.001
I felt other churchgoers were attending church for the wrong reasons	46	29	.01
I felt other churchgoers were not authentic Christians	33	19	.01

In order to understand more about the way in which the values of the church leavers under the age of 50 differed from the values of the church leavers aged 50 and over, we turned to a different section of the questionnaire. This time we predicted that those under the age of 50 would place more emphasis on counter-cultural values. The findings from this comparison are summarized in Table 14.2. Once again these data demonstrate that our predictions were generally confirmed.

Conclusion

In this paper I have touched on just a few of the far-reaching shifts that have occurred in cultural values over the last four decades. I have suggested that rather than losing their faith, the church leavers under the age of 50 may have adopted a *different* style of faith, less conducive to churchgoing, in response to these cultural shifts. People born since 1946 tend to be a 'generation of seekers', with a distinctive set of values. They have an intrinsic tendency to be suspicious of all institutions, including the church; they are drawn to more mystical beliefs,

Table 14.2 Counter-cultural values by age group

	under 50 %	50 and over %	p <
Respondents would welcome:			
more emphasis on self-expression	64	48	.01
more acceptance of sexual freedom	52	15	.001
less emphasis on working hard	33	18	.01
more acceptance of marijuana usage	34	10	.001
Respondents would not welcome:			
more emphasis on traditional family ties	20	4	.001
more respect for authority	21	6	.001

they prioritize experience above belief, and they tend to 'shop around' widely to satisfy their needs for personal authenticity and spiritual growth. As we have seen, church leaving by those born since 1946 can only be fully understood in this context. There are other complementary frameworks of interpretation (for instance, the dynamics of the leaving process) but the context and strength of this theme in the accounts given by our interviewees does suggest that nowadays cultural changes have put a premium on the safeguarding of personal authenticity. This, in turn, suggests that the attribution of membership decline to, for example, inappropriate worship styles may be misguided. What may ultimately matter is for churches to honour that quest for personal authenticity.

References

Coupland, D. (1992), *Generation X: Tales for an Accelerated Culture*, London, Abacus Books.

Hoge, D. R. (1981), *Converts Dropouts Returnees: A Study of Religious Change among Catholics*, New York, Pilgrim Press.

Richter, P. and Francis, L. J. (1998), *Gone But Not Forgotten: Church Leaving and Returning in the Twenty-First Century*, London, Darton, Longman & Todd.

Ritchie, K. (1995), *Marketing to Generation X*, New York, Lexington.

Roof, W. C. (1993), *A Generation of Seekers: The Spiritual Journeys of the Baby Boom Generation*, San Francisco, Harper.

Roof, W C. and Johnson, M. (1993), Baby boomers and the return to the churches, in D. A. Roozen and C. Kirk Hadaway (eds), *Church and Denominational Growth: What Does (and Does not) Cause Growth or Decline*, pp. 293–310, Nashville, Abingdon Press.
Troeltsch, E. (1931), *The Social Teachings of the Christian Churches*, London, George Allen and Unwin.

15

Gay and Lesbian Christians: The Lived Experiences

Andrew K. T. Yip

Introduction

The twentieth-anniversary celebration of the Lesbian and Gay Christian Movement (LGCM) at Southwark Cathedral, London, on 16 November 1996 was surrounded by highly-publicized controversy. While supporters rejoiced at the resilience and achievement of this movement, despite the lack of social support and religious affirmation, critics expressed dismay at the use of the Cathedral for 'the celebration of 20 years of gay sex'. Controversy of this nature surfaced once again during the Lambeth Conference in July/August 1998. What such controversy certainly manifests is that the Christian community is as divided as ever on the contentious issue of homosexuality. This is not surprising, as sex and sexuality are issues with which Christianity has never been at ease.

In this chapter, I share my observations of this debate and some findings of the sociological research I have undertaken on gay and lesbian Christians in Britain. Here, I focus on two studies: first, a quantitative and qualitative study on the dynamics of 68 gay male Christian partnerships; second, a postal membership survey commissioned by Quest (the national organization for gay and lesbian Catholics with a membership of approximately 400), in which 121 participated.

Combining religion and homosexuality is still a rare effort in sociological research. Sociology of religion, for instance, has largely focused on religious institutions, ideas and forms. In spite of an increasing call for a shift of paradigm which gives greater weight to religious experiences (for example, Spickard, 1993; Roof, 1996), the new framework has not been extended to gay and lesbian believers, who constitute a largely hidden segment of the Christian community.

Widening chasm

Almost all the literature available on gay and lesbian Christians is written within a theological framework (with the exception of, for example, Fletcher, 1990; O'Brien, 1991; Thumma, 1991). This is unsurprising, since the Bible is the primary, though not the exclusive, basis that shapes the churches' responses to homosexuality. Thus, biblical exegesis forms the core of the moral-religious discourse of homosexuality, in which various churches have embroiled themselves in the past two decades.

Brash (1995) and Hertman (1996) have provided a good overview of the various churches' official positions on this thorny issue. I shall focus, in this chapter, on the Roman Catholic Church and the Church of England. Moralistic vocabulary suggestive of personal pathology used by the Roman Catholic Church in labelling the homosexual orientation an 'objective disorder' and same-sex genital acts 'intrinsically disordered' (for example, Congregation for the Doctrine of the Faith, 1986) expectedly provoke impassioned reaction from gay and lesbian Catholics. For instance, 84 per cent of the gay and lesbian Catholics I surveyed considered the Catholic Church's official positions in this respect 'unconvincing' or 'very unconvincing'; 85 per cent argued that the Church should refrain from using such negative language; 91 per cent asserted that absolutions should not be sought when same-sex genital acts are committed within a faithful and committed partnership, thus implying that the practice of homosexuality within the context of a partnership is morally compatible with their Catholic faith (for more details see Yip, 1996a, 1997a).

In contrast, the Church of England has been more actively engaged in the debate on homosexuality (see Coleman, 1989). It seemed to have taken a welcoming step forward with the House of Bishops' publication, *Issues in Human Sexuality* (Church of England, 1991), in which congregations were encouraged to accept gay and lesbian laity who, having searched their Christian conscience, decided to be in same-sex partnerships that involved the full expression of their sexuality. This measure, however, does not extend to gay clergy primarily because of their profession. Such double standards have attracted much criticism (for example, Sumners, 1995). A respondent who participated in my study on gay male Christian couples (Yip, 1997b) represented many when he asserted:

> So now they say it's all right if you are a lay person to have a homosexual relationship although it falls short of the ideal ... [but] it is not all right if you are a priest to have a sexual relationship. Does that mean to say that laity are somehow second-rate Christians to clergy? I mean it's quite absurd theologically speaking.

Indisputably, there exists a chasm between the churches' official positions and the lived experiences of gay and lesbian Christians who, despite the lack of religious affirmation and institutional support, remain in the churches or still keep their Christian faith despite having physically distanced themselves from the churches. This chasm is certainly widening as the churches move forward at a snail's pace, and the gay and lesbian Christian community is becoming increasingly confident and influential in rattling the cage of religious orthodoxy (Comstock, 1996).

Within the theological sphere itself, there has been a burgeoning corpus of gay- and lesbian-affirming literature in the past two decades constituting a strong reverse discourse which increasingly weakens the moral authority and intellectual rigour of the churches' dominant discourse (for example, Boswell, 1980; McNeill, 1988; Nelson and Longfellow, 1994; Vasey, 1995; Seow, 1996). Besides challenging specifically the churches' conventional interpretation of the scriptures on homosexuality, this body of theological literature also repudiates the line of demarcation the churches draw between homosexual orientation and practice: that a person with a homosexual orientation should not be discriminated against, but the practice of this orientation is incompatible with the Christian faith. This principle is rejected on the ground that it focuses on sexual *acts*, rather than *relationships*. Supportive theologians have argued that the churches' 'theology of sexual acts' must give way to a 'theology of relationships' that emphasizes inter-partner mutuality, relationality, emotional commitment, instead of what people do in bed. In the case of intimate relationships for instance, the sexual quality and not the sexual form should be the criterion for evaluation (for example, Ellison, 1990; John, 1993; Boswell, 1994). Stuart (1995, 1996) went further by arguing for a 'theology of friendship', equipped with an apparent ideology of egalitarianism and inclusiveness, as the model for all kinds of human relationships.

Listening to lived experiences

It is heartening to observe that gay- and lesbian-affirming theology is gaining strength in the debate. Nevertheless, I would like to suggest that in order to consider the issue of homosexuality more effectively and productively, the churches need to incorporate into the hitherto theological debate the lived experiences of gay and lesbian Christians. How do gay and lesbian Christians experience God? How do they interpret the traditionally perceived biblical injunctions against same-sex genital acts? How do they organize their spirituality despite the lack of institutional support? How do they rationalize their life-worlds? These are but a few of the questions whose answers the churches must be committed to finding.

To achieve this, the churches, as Nelson (1992, p. 21) argued, need to relinquish a 'theology of sexuality' and practise a 'sexual theology' instead. The former approach uses scriptures and tradition literally to inform our understanding of sexuality. The latter approach emphasizes the use of lived experiences as the starting point for our understanding of scriptures and tradition. To practise the latter, the churches need to listen, and listen attentively.

To this end, sociological research makes its contribution by providing insights into the lived experiences and biographical narratives of gay and lesbian Christians. This is relevant because not giving the space and voice for this little-known segment of the Christian community to speak safely would render the debate an intellectualizing process without a human face. In addition, the parallels that we can draw between gay- and lesbian-affirming theology and sociological evidence of their lived experiences would help construct a broader and more wholesome framework for the debate.

In this connection, the 'theology of relationships' is echoed in the sociological discourse of homosexuality. Weeks (1995, p. 54), for instance, argued that the conceptualization of postmodern morality requires us to shift away 'from a morality of acts, which locates truth and rightness or wrongdoing in particular practices, and the expression of creation desires, and towards an ethics of relationships, and choice of relationships, which is intent on listening to how we engage with one another, and respond to one another's needs as fellow human beings'. Weeks proposed what he called 'radical humanism', with care, respect, responsibility and knowledge as its core elements, as the way ahead in the face of sexual pluralism in postmodern society.

The findings of my own research seem to suggest that the credibility of the churches and the validity of their official positions are indeed under rigorous scrutiny and challenge. Gay and lesbian Christians, drawing upon their own positive experiences that attest to the compatibility and possibility of being homosexual and Christian, are becoming more vocal and assertive, therefore less willing to be silenced by social censure (Yip, 1997c, 1999). This reliance on personal experiences is clearly manifested in the following account by a respondent in the study on gay male Christian couples:

> I endeavour to be a Christian and I try to incorporate Christian principles into my life. It has got to influence the way I live with [his partner], the way I treat [his partner]. When we had problems in the relationship, I prayed for the relationship, and eventually things had been improved. And that's what made me convinced in myself. I have received help in this relationship when we needed it. If what we are doing is totally against God, he wouldn't have answered my prayers.

As the gay- and lesbian-affirming theologians have argued, the traditionally perceived biblical prohibition that a man

191

should not lie with another man because it is an abomination; or the frequently-used 'against nature' argument conceptualizes homosexuality within a context of isolated sexual acts. It is a reductionist conceptualization of gay and lesbian sexuality as mere non-procreative genitalization, against the perceived norm of heterosexual marital intercourse. It does not take into consideration the context of a faithful and committed relationship in which the partners' Christian faith can be affirmed. Another respondent who participated in the study on gay male Christian couples asserted in support of this argument:

> The homosexuality ... that existed during the Old Testament times and New Testament times was probably very different from the sort of relationships that exist now. Paul particularly is writing about gay prostitution in Corinthians. [The Bible] wasn't against the homosexuality that has developed in loving relationships. It doesn't seem that it's loving relationships that is under attack in scriptures. A loving relationship is immensely positive, enriching and Christian.

This 'theology of relationships' is also emphasized by most of the gay and lesbian Catholics who participated in the membership survey. The following are two typical accounts:

> In my view there is morality between all sexual activity within a faithful, committed and monogamous relationship between two people of any gender regardless of whether or not it has received the stamp of approval from [the] church and [the] state.

> God created us in his own image, homosexual. He doesn't make mistakes. Our essential Christian vocation is the same as everyone else's, to receive love and to give love. Most human beings are clearly called to a loving sexual, one-to-one relationship with another. We are, too. It is our duty to fulfil our vocation to give love and to receive love in stable relationships. The church is quite wrong in what it

says about this, and doing severe damage to the Body of Christ.

Admittedly, the sociological and theological exploration for new paradigms or ethics within a virtual normative vacuum is not without its challenges. Within the gay and lesbian Christian community specifically, there exists a diversity of views in relation to some fundamental issues such as same-sex marriage, sexual exclusivity within partnership, and the youth- and physique-oriented gay sub-culture (see, for example, Williams, 1990; John, 1993; Stuart 1995; Yip, 1996b, 1996c, 1997d). This is an indication of an increasingly diversified agenda. I personally view this development in a positive light, despite the surmountable difficulty it currently presents. This development is evidence that the gay and lesbian [Christian] community has moved further away from the 'justification stage' in their personal and collective identity development. It is a welcoming indication that diverse and competing perspectives are given space to participate in the debate, potentially leading to 'more and more ways of thinking about same-sex sexualities and relationships that do not lock us up in controlling categories, but which instead empower us towards difference and diversity' (Plummer, 1992, p. 15).

It is undeniable that the churches cannot insulate themselves behind religious rhetoric and tradition. In order to reach out effectively to gay and lesbian Christians, a theological approach must be coupled with a sociological awareness about their lived experiences. Religious institutions are traditionally concerned with monolithic religious dogma and moral absolutes as timeless truths. But the tide of social change is against this, for post-modernity represents a culture of difference and diversity. People with dissident sexual identities are becoming less accepting of the hegemony of compulsory heterosexuality and being defined within the framework of heteronormativity. Therefore, they are more vocal about their presence within the churches, seeking a share of their sexual citizenship in humanity. Not heeding this trend of diversity, the churches would, to use Marx's words slightly out of context, 'sow its own seed of destruction'.

Ironically, the decline of the churches as a social institution need not lead to a process of 'despiritualization' in individuals.

193

In fact, it might give rise to more fluid and dynamic religious styles and experiences, as people in the consumerist 1990s increasingly use their personal experiences and biographical narratives as the starting point of spirituality and the basis for the construction of their 'sacred cosmos', instead of uncritically subscribing to grand theological systems (Roof, 1993).

To conclude, the growing confidence of the gay and lesbian Christian community should gradually compel the churches to shift their paradigm in the examination of homosexuality. The actual lived experiences of people who are the thrust of the debate should be given space and a voice. Thus, the theological debate cannot insulate itself within the familiar biblical vocabulary of morality. It must incorporate into it the lived experiences of gay and lesbian Christians. This might well serve as an opportunity for churches to learn about the importance of recognizing the diversity of human experiences in our 'postparadigmatic society' (Simon, 1996, p. 9), where pluralism gradually leads to the dissolution of grand paradigms of consensual social meanings, and lived experiences increasingly become the basis for the construction of personal identity.

References

Boswell, J. (1980), *Christianity, Social Tolerance and Homosexuality*, Chicago, University of Chicago Press.

Boswell, J. (1994), *Same-Sex Unions in Premodern Europe*, New York, Villard.

Brash, A. (1995), *Facing our Differences: The Churches and their Gay and Lesbian Members*, Geneva, World Council of Churches.

Church of England (1991), *Issues in Human Sexuality: A Statement by the House of Bishops*, London, Church House Publishing.

Coleman, P. (1989), *Gay Christian: A Moral Dilemma*, London, SCM Press.

Comstock, G. D. (1996), *Unrepentant, Self-Affirming, Practicing: Lesbian/Bisexual/Gay People within Organized Religion*, New York, Continuum.

Congregation for the Doctrine of the Faith (1986), *Letter to the Bishops of the Catholic Church on the Pastoral Care of Homosexual Persons*, London, Catholic Truth Society.

Ellison, M. (1990), Common decency: a new Christian sexual ethics, *Christianity and Crisis*, 12, 352–6.

Gay and Lesbian Christians

Fletcher, B. C. (1990), *Clergy Under Stress: A Study of Homosexual and Heterosexual Clergy in the Church of England*, London, Mowbray.

Hertman, K. (1996), *Congregations in Conflict: The Battle over Homosexuality*, New Brunswick, New Jersey, Rutgers University Press.

John, J. (1993), *Permanent, Faithful, Stable: Christian Same-Sex Partnerships*, London, Affirming Catholicism.

McNeill, J. J. (1988) (3rd edn), *The Church and the Homosexual*, Boston, Beacon Press.

Nelson, J. B. (1992), *Body Theology*, Louisville, Westminster John Knox Press.

Nelson, J. B. and Longfellow, S. P. (eds) (1994), *Sexuality and the Sacred: Sources for Theological Reflection*, Louisville, Westminster John Knox Press.

O'Brien, T. (1991), A survey of gay/lesbian Catholics concerning attitudes toward sexual orientation and religious beliefs, *Journal of Homosexuality*, 21, 29–44.

Plummer, K. (ed.) (1992), *Modern Homosexualities: Fragments of Lesbian and Gay Experiences*, London, Routledge.

Roof, W. C. (1993), *A Generation of Seekers: The Spiritual Journeys of the Baby Boom Generation*, New York, HarperCollins.

Roof, W. C. (1996), God is in the details: reflections on religion's public presence in the United States in the mid-1990s, *Sociology of Religion*, 57, 149–62.

Seow, C. L. (1996), *Homosexuality and Christian Community*, Louisville, Westminster John Knox Press.

Simon, W. (1996), *Postmodern Sexualities*, London, Routledge.

Spickard, J. V. (1993), For a sociology of religious experience, in W. H. Swatos Jr. (ed.), *A Future for Religion? New Paradigms for Social Analysis*, pp. 109–28, Newbury Park, Sage.

Stuart, E. (1995), *Just Good Friends: Towards a Lesbian and Gay Theology of Relationships*, London, Mowbray.

Stuart, E. (1996), Lesbian and gay relationships: a lesbian feminist perspective, in E. Stuart and A. Thatcher (eds), *Christian Perspectives on Sexuality and Gender*, pp. 301–17, Leominster, Gracewing.

Sumners, C. (ed.) (1995), *Reconsider: A Response to Issues in Human Sexuality*, London, Lesbian and Gay Christian Movement.

Thumma, S. (1991), Negotiating a religious identity: the case of the gay evangelicals, *Sociological Analysis*, 52, 333–47.

Vasey, M. (1995), *Strangers and Friends: A New Exploration of Homosexuality and the Bible*, London, Hodder & Stoughton.

Weeks, J. (1995), *Invented Moralities*, Cambridge, Polity Press.

Williams, R. (1990), Toward a theology of lesbian and gay marriage, *Anglican Theological Review*, 72, 134–57.

Yip, A. K. T. (1996a), Quest membership survey report [edited version], *The Month: A Review of Christian Thought and World Affairs*, 29, 439–45.

Yip, A. K. T. (1996b), Gay Christians and their participation in the gay subculture, *Deviant Behavior*, 17, 297–318.

Yip, A. K. T. (1996c), Gay Christian couples and blessing ceremonies, *Theology and Sexuality*, 4, 101–17.

Yip, A. K. T. (1997a), Dare to differ: gay and lesbian Catholics' assessment of the official Catholic positions on sexuality, *Sociology of Religion*, 58, 165–80.

Yip, A. K. T. (1997b), *Gay Male Christian Couples: Life Stories*, Westport, Connecticut, Praeger.

Yip, A. K. T. (1997c), Attacking the attacker: gay Christians talk back, *British Journal of Sociology*, 48, 113–27.

Yip, A. K. T. (1997d), Gay male Christian couples and sexual exclusivity, *Sociology*, 31, 289–306.

Yip, A. K. T. (1999), The politics of counter-rejection: gay Christians and the Church, *Journal of Homosexuality*, (in press).

16

Developing Identity as a Local Non-stipendiary Priest

Michael West

Introduction

Ordained Local Ministry (OLM), until recently more commonly known as Local Non-Stipendiary Ministry (LNSM), is an unpaid clergy ministry, exercised in a local situation which is both its principle source of vocation and its principle source of training. Members of local congregations who feel called to clergy ministry are able, through the development of OLM, to test a vocation to priesthood which has emerged through their association with the local church, be trained locally, be ordained by the bishop and then work as an assistant priest in that same local parish or benefice. The Church of England Advisory Board for Ministry (1991) identified it as a catholic order in the service of the local church, set in the context of collaborative ministerial practice, requiring a commitment to working in teams.

The present study of OLM, reported further by West (1995), can accurately be described as a 'case study set within a naturalistic research paradigm'. Identified as an umbrella to cover a diverse range of research methodologies (Simons, 1987), 'naturalistic research' involves the use of qualitative research methodology and represents a commitment to innovative change through the provision of new insights into the issues and dilemmas of the research process and the provision and evaluation of practical strategies for their resolution and development.

The research sought to identify the issues and dilemmas raised by training individuals for Ordained Local Ministry and Accredited Ministry in the local church situation through a case study of three groups in the Diocese of St Edmundsbury and Ipswich which were undertaking a pilot scheme for OLM and then subsequently through the biographical study of eight individuals from those groups who had been selected for training as OLMs. It then sought to place these issues and dilemmas within the contexts of the recent history and present experience of the Church of England and the social constructions of what Giddens (1990, pp. 45–53) identifies as 'high' modernity. An important focus of the study was the identity and ministerial development of the OLMs and this forms the context of this article.

Identity formation emerged as a key issue from the first research cycle for the groups and the individuals. In order to identify categories for the different elements that may be active in this process, I turned initially to Knowles' (1992, p. 114) 'Biographical Transformation' model. Knowles identified four major components in teacher role identity formation that he argues are evidenced by his case studies: childhood experiences, teacher role models, teacher experiences and significant or important prior experiences or relationships. The 'Biographical Transformation' model was designed to generate theory about the relationship between the individual teacher's biography and their current teacher practice. This model seemed to provide data that would illuminate the process of clergy role identity formation.

Using the model required engagement with 'Life history' research to produce a 'life-history' narrative for each of the trainee OLMs, to describe the practice and context of each individual's present ministerial experience, and to attempt to establish formative links between the two. I collected data about the individual's life-history through an exercise developed by the Centre for Faith Development entitled 'The Unfolding Tapestry of my Life' and followed this with two sets of interviews. I employed content analysis (McKernan, 1991) to identify different categories within the discourse.

In order to explore the individuals' present experience I asked each of the students to keep a 'journal' as a study in reflective, analytical writing. I also undertook two 'case study' group exercises, based on the kind of pastoral situations that they were bound to encounter in their everyday ministries, designed to identify beliefs and values that are realized in action and observable in the decision making process (see Elliott, 1993). I also collected data through a comprehensive questionnaire designed to elicit details about the individuals' current practice, the training programme and the significant positive and negative contexts in which they operated.

The 'Biographical Transformation' model provided an important set of categories and connections that helped illuminate clergy identity formation through making important connections between biography and present experience. However, my own data do not support Knowles' assertion that the model is an accurate representation of the relationship. Knowles (1992, p. 139) recognizes that 'There is not merely a cause and effect relationship; instead, biography interacts with the context and experiences of teaching in a variety of ways that may be difficult to determine.' I recognized that the complexity of the relationship between biography and present experience was more appropriately represented in narrative form as this can better express truth claims that are open and tentative. I therefore created narratives in collaboration with each of the eight individuals. They were composed using data grounded in the students' accounts and provided a summary of the research findings as they related to each individual. The following areas of significance emerged from the study.

Significance of life-history experience

Life-history data from the study suggest that the beliefs, values, attitudes and agendas that are formed through biographical experience exercise a powerful influence on ministerial formation and practice. Data further confirmed that individuals experience this formation through both a continuity of experience and processes of discontinuity and transition. These categories were initially employed as a means of organizing the students' life-history data to conceptualize the changes that they had experienced and to investigate how these might affect their current practice. However, it became clear that continuity, discontinuity and transition affected every aspect of the way that the students conceived their lives. Two had each

constructed a life-history narrative around significant continuities of experience. Both had retired, both had enjoyed long
and successful careers and both had enjoyed stable long-term
relationships with wives and children. Both came from secure
homes and the value positions taught to them by their parents
had been instrumental in the way that they have constructed
and developed their own family lives. Both established the
pattern of their church lives early, both became Readers a few
years ago and both believe that their ordination confirms a
ministry that has been in place for some time. Although
exhibiting moments of minor discontinuity and transition, the
narratives confirm that their current values, beliefs, attitudes
and agendas have been slowly developing over a period of
many years.

In contrast, three others constructed life-history narratives
that hinge on significant moments of transition when beliefs,
values, attitudes and agendas became subject to change and
development. One person identifies her divorce as a powerful
discontinuity and her subsequent remarriage as an important
transition. Three individuals identified a powerful 'born again'
experience which led to a radical discontinuity and transition of
core beliefs, values, attitudes and agendas. One further exhibits
a period of discontinuity and transition in his family and work
experience.

The narratives constructed by the other three show examples
of both kinds of experience. There are clear examples of their
family, church and work experience being subject to both
continuity and also discontinuity and transition. In each case
both kinds of experience are important, but neither is
overridingly significant in the overall narrative.

The narratives further suggested that for some people role
models have been an important influence on their lives,
explaining how certain values were received. One identified
two curates who, he believed, had helped him to recognize the
need to be both 'one of the boys' and 'challenging' in his
ministry. Another identified a clergyman who had an enormous
influence on her life as tutor on her counselling course. She
appears to have recognized the course's core values in his own
person.

For others, role models appeared not to have been
particularly significant in their life-history narrative and

appeared rather to reinforce the values that were already prevalent within the biographical project. One identified two clergy who were 'sensitive' and 'patient', qualities that he has recently come to respect and attempt to cultivate. Another identified two clergy who loved people and evangelized by the way that they led their lives, two themes that he recognizes as being in place within his own life experience well before he encountered the individuals concerned.

Church context

The local church provides the focal arena in which clergy ministry is set. It touches both the aspirations of the ministers themselves and the expectations of the church officials and members whom they encounter. Each individual identified strongly with a metaphor for priesthood and there was a clear correlation between these metaphors and the activities that they undertook within the church. One individual's identity as 'shepherd' and 'priest' is supported by a strong pastoral, liturgical and teaching ministry and a positive role in the church's committee structure. Another's identity as a 'pastor', 'bridge builder' and 'practical carer' is supported by a strong pastoral ministry.

The expectations of others in the church context were also of great significance. Indeed, in one important sense the expectations of a variety of key people and groups of people can legitimately be seen as the backdrop to the whole process of the development of local ministry. These have been part and parcel of the way that clergy, PCCs, individuals, the bishop, the diocese and the broader church have developed the scheme that has enabled individuals to be selected and to train in the locations that have formed the basis of this study. However, this study attempted to identify the expectations that individuals within their local church context have perceived to have affected the development of their clergy role identities.

By and large individuals coped with these expectations on the basis of their reasonableness. They did not feel that it was reasonable to expect them to be available all the time or to expect them to know everything or not exhibit weakness. Therefore these expectations were met by the development of appropriate coping strategies and did not challenge the constructions of their clergy role identities. However, in one case the congregation expectations did appear to be reasonable and did challenge one individual's construction of his clergy role identity. One individual admitted that the congregation's expectation of him as a pastor and counsellor had challenged his previous role identity as teacher and administrator and was responsible for him attempting to reconstruct his parish role.

Family context

Even though six individuals experienced difficulty in freeing sufficient time for the enjoyment of family life, and for four of these this was a major issue, a very high value was placed on family life. All eight individuals strongly associated with the role of mother/father and wife/husband, and although one argued that Christ came first in his house and that his wife agreed with this, all others placed the family before any other church or work commitment.

There was also a strong correlation between the roles that individuals adopted in their homes and the roles that they were constructing in the church context. One's motherly role in the church reflected her traditional role as mother and housewife at home. The context of equality and mutual decision-making that another experienced at home matched her role as emancipator and democrat in the church.

Work context

Two of the students were recently retired and two were housewives. However, the other four, who were in full-time work at the start of this study, were experiencing conflict and concern within the work environment. One is looking to reduce the hours that he spends at work to concentrate more fully on his church ministry, and another sees his career as a constant source of conflict because of his faith. Another feels that he has had a good career but that he is now increasingly at odds with his firm's macho management style and is therefore vulnerable to redundancy. Indeed, it is clear that those involved in constructing a clergy role identity while undertaking full or part-time work experienced certain levels of conflict between the two activities and that all failed to draw on their work experience to help support their ministerial development.

Both the close association between clergy role identity and the home environment, and the conflict between clergy role identity and the workplace, may well find a broader context in what Moody (1992) identifies as the privatization of religion. In late modernity religion has increasingly become associated with the realm of private choice and personal activity and the work place has become associated with a public sphere which is both secularized and driven by its own appropriate technical rationality. Religious identity has been increasingly restricted to individual relationships, the home, and particular religious institutions. Also, Church of England groups as diverse as the Mothers' Union, the Board for Social Responsibility and the Liturgical Commission have all emphasized the value of Christian 'family life' in the last two decades and have increasingly projected the church community as a 'family' unit. This has further cemented the close association between church and family institutions.

Broader societal contexts

Two broad societal contexts, those of class and gender, were identified in the research process. They are both deeply embedded cultural contexts that are influential factors that help construct the past and the present. They therefore affect issues of life-history as well as those of present context.

Class was envisaged in terms of 'consciousness communities' (Crompton, 1993). Although it is difficult to ascertain which class index individuals may have in mind when identifying their own class (although employment categories may well be significant in this context), there are ample examples of attitudes to employment, education, gender and morality within the life-history narratives that suggest the influence of a 'consciousness community' set in a particular historical and geographical context.

The historical and geographical contexts into which each individual was born differed significantly. The influences of these different contexts are clearly delineated in the individual life-history narratives and surface particularly around their differing attitudes to education, employment, gender and morality, providing strong evidence to suggest that each of the students has retained strong links with their initial 'consciousness communities' and that these continue to play an important role in the construction of their clergy role identity.

Gender issues encompass life-history experience and current context, as well as wider perspectives both within the Anglican Church and within society at large. The feminist perspective is becoming increasingly well established in the arts and social sciences, and within the Anglican Church women have been admitted to priesthood within the life span of this study. This gender issue had two aspects. The first relates to the way that gender affects the construction of clergy role identities of men and women. The fact that men's ministry still constitutes the norm in the church community means that gender issues were more visible in the lives and ministries of women. In fact the experience of the three women is diverse. As a qualified counsellor one brings creative pastoral skills to her ministry. She feels fully accepted in her constructed role of priest/ mediator in her local church community. Another has attempted initially to create a role of mother/pastor in the local church community. Calling herself 'conventional' and liking 'the man to lead' she has found pastoral work rewarding but has struggled to have her authority recognized in leadership tasks traditionally associated with male authority. The third has been a feminist from her university days and associates herself with the feminist theological critique of church life. She is constructing a clergy role identity in the context of her desire to enable women to be fully emancipated into church life.

Although the 'maleness' of the clergy role identity constructed by the men is more difficult to identify, three of the men employ images of a priesthood in which a strong male identity combines with a clear sense of their own authority and ministry within the local church and within broader church structures.

Henrietta Santer (1984) argues that there are generally agreed 'masculine' and 'feminine' characteristics or personal attributes within the church. Feminine attributes are identified as affectionate, warm, dependent, sensitive and caring, and masculine attributes are identified as independent, assertive, dominant, competitive and forceful. These culturally defined attributes have a history in church life and experience and have been implicit in this study at many points. Each of the students made the gender assumption that women would be good at pastoral matters and men at administration and leading worship and most struggled with what they identified as the 'masculine' and 'feminine' within themselves. Therefore, although the gender issue can be identified in the activities and aspirations that separate women from men, it can also be identified in the internal struggles that affect the role construction of both men and women, especially within a church culture that both discriminates against women and yet values the feminine highly.

Theological context: vocation

The word 'vocation' places the individual's perceptions of ministry within a theological framework that draws from the tradition of the church, where 'vocation' focuses a relationship in which the individual discerns God's will and then responds through an act of service. It reflects the dynamic of 'call and response' which is often conceived as basic to the salvific relationship between God and the individual (see McFadyen, 1990). The selection of an individual for clergy ministry is therefore designed to reflect this theological process of call, discernment and response.

Each student recognized this vocation but understood its roots to lie in different contexts of their life-history experience. Two of the men envisaged their vocation emerging from the continuity of experience and service that had taken a lifetime to develop and had been previously manifested in readership training. Others came to vocation through the transitional experience of being 'born again' and one came to priestly vocation unexpectedly having joined the ministry team with the intention of training for other forms of accredited ministry. Notions of 'vocation' conceived in this way clearly constituted an important element in the construction of clergy role identity in the present contexts of their ministries as well as to the way in which individuals felt their clergy role identity would be constructed in the future.

Conclusion

This research identifies and acknowledges the key role played by the various contexts in which ministry is exercised, but

Michael West

suggests that the individual's life-history is a prominent influence on the construction of clergy role identity. Beliefs, values, attitudes and agendas that are forged in the 'consciousness communities' of early experience and informed by gender and church experience are subject to the continuities, discontinuities and transitions of the individual's biography and emerge to inform ministerial practice. Hence the three individuals who have worked together as a ministry team in the same church for a significant period of time, and have therefore enjoyed similar contexts for the development of their ministerial roles, have each constructed a very different clergy role identity.

References

Advisory Board for Ministry (1991), *Policy Paper 1 Local NSM*, London, Church House Publishing.

Crompton, R. (1993), *Class and Stratification*, Cambridge, Polity Press.

Elliott, J. (1993), *Constructing Teacher Education*, London, Falmer Press.

Giddens, A. (1990), *The Consequences of Modernity*, Cambridge, Polity Press.

Knowles, J. G. (1992), Models for understanding pre-service and beginning teachers' biographies, in I. Goodson (ed.), *Studying Teachers' Lives*, London, Routledge, pp. 51–99.

McFadyen, A. (1990), *The Call to Personhood*, Cambridge, Cambridge University Press.

McKernan, J. (1991), *Curriculum Action Research*, London, Kogan Page.

Moody, C. (1992), *Eccentric Ministry: Pastoral Care and Leadership* in the Church, London, Darton, Longman & Todd.

Santer, H. (1984), Stereotyping the sexes in society and in the church, in M. Furlong (ed.), *Feminine in the Church*, pp. 139–49, London, SPCK.

Simons, H. (1987), *Getting to Know Schools in a Democracy: The Politics and Process of Evaluation*, London, Falmer Press.

West, M. (1995), *Second Class Priests with Second Class Training? A Study of Local Non-Stipendiary Ministry in the Church of England Diocese of St Edmundsbury and Ipswich,* Unpublished PhD dissertation, University of East Anglia.

Name Index

207

Name Index

Name Index

Larson, D.B.   117, 123
Lash, N.   29, 46, 83, 91
Lawless, E.   44, 47
Leclercq, J.   79–80
Lee, R.M.   167, 174
Lenin, V.I.   11
Lennon, J.   26
Leone, M.   94, 103
Lerner, D.   47
Lester, D.   146, 153
Levine, D.   2, 47
Levitt, M.   156–157, 159, 164
Levy, D.   43, 47
Lewis, I.M.   23, 47
Lewis, J.M.   93, 102, 146, 153
Libânio, J.B.   63, 71
Longfellow, S.P.   189, 195
Longfield, B.   4, 47
Louden, L.M.R.   145, 154
Lovekin, A.A.   125, 133
Luckmann, T.   23, 45, 47, 165–166, 174
Lukes, S.   36, 47

McCullough, M.E.   117, 123
McFadyen, A.   205–206
Macfarlane, A.   10
McGavran, D.   136, 142–143
McGee, G.B.   136, 143
McGregor, G.P.   145, 154
MacIntyre, A.   17, 46–47
McKernan, J.   198, 206
McLellan, D.   65, 71
McLeod, H.   33
McNeill, J.J.   189, 195
Malony, H.N.   125, 133
Mandela, N.   11
Mannheim, K.   47, 71
Markham, I.   47
Marsden, G.   4, 47
Martin, B.   25, 47, 168, 174
Martin, D.   1, 20, 39, 47–48, 50–51,
   55–56, 60, 68, 71, 93–94, 102
Marty, M.   46
Marx, K.   59, 71–72, 75, 77–78, 83–84,
   91, 105, 163
Matthews, D.A.   117, 123, 176–177,
   179–180
Mauss, A.   95–96, 102
May, P.   170, 174
May, T.   127–129, 131, 133
Mead, G.H.   48
Medhurst, K.   32, 48
Middlemiss, D.   89, 91
Milano, M.G.   117, 123
Milbank, J.   43, 48, 55, 57, 60, 67, 71, 85,
   87, 91
Miller, A.S.   117, 123

Mills, C.W.   23, 48
Mintz, S.   48
Mitchell, B.   17, 48, 71
Moody, C.   203, 206
More, C.   145, 154
Morris, P.   29, 46
Moyser, G.   32, 48
Mullen, K.   114, 116–117, 123
Musgrave, A.   8, 42, 47
Mutli, K.   155, 164

Nash, A.   60
Naylor, L.   145, 154
Nelson, J.B.   189–190, 195
Neuhaus, R.   17
Newbiggin, L.   105, 112
Newby, H.   89, 91
Niebuhr, H.R.   108, 112
Niebuhr, R.   108, 112
Norman, E.   147, 154
Norussis, M.   139, 143

O'Brien, T.   188, 195
O'Dea, T.   32, 87, 91
Oss, D.A.   136, 143

Parsons, T.   23
Percy, M.   82, 84, 87–88, 90, 92, 98, 102
Perrin, R.   95–96, 99, 102
Perry, P.E.   117, 124, 146–147, 149, 154
Philipchalk, R.   146, 153–154
Phillips, D.Z.   70–71
Piaget, J.   17
Pickering, W.S.F.   36, 48
Pluck, R.   168, 174
Plummer, K.   193, 195
Polanyi, M.   42, 48
Poloma, M.M.   99, 102, 125, 133, 137,
   141–142, 144
Popper, K.   42, 48
Poythress, V.S.   125–126, 134
Preston, R.   50

Ramsey, P.   17
Reed, B.   106, 109, 112
Rex, R.   35
Richter, P.   175–176, 185
Ricoeur, P.   25, 48
Ritchie, K.   177, 185
Robbins, M.   145–146, 154
Robertson, R.   20, 48
Robinson, M.   173–174
Roof, W.C.   176–177, 179, 181–182,
   185–186, 188, 194–195
Roozen, D.A.   186
Rose, J.   31, 48
Rose, M.   145, 154

209

Subject Index